# The American Destiny

*Volume 4*

## The American Character

# The American Destiny

## An Illustrated Bicentennial History of the United States

Editor in Chief
**Henry Steele Commager**

Editors
**Marcus Cunliffe**
**Maldwyn A. Jones**
**Edward Horton**

The Danbury Press

EDITOR IN CHIEF: Henry Steele Commager has taught history at Columbia, Cambridge, Oxford, and other universities, and at Amherst College, for over forty years. He is the coauthor (with S. E. Morison) of *The Growth of the American Republic,* and author of *Theodore Parker, The American Mind, Majority Rule and Minority Rights,* and many other books. He is the editor of *Documents of American History* and, with Richard B. Morris, of the fifty-volume *New American Nation Series.* Professor Commager was recently awarded the Gold Medal of the American Academy of Arts and Letters for his historical writings.

SENIOR EDITORS: Marcus Cunliffe is Professor of American Studies at the University of Sussex. He has been a Commonwealth Fellow at Yale and has taught at Harvard and other American universities. Professor Cunliffe's books include *The Literature of the United States, The Nation Takes Shape, Soldiers and Civilians,* and *The American Presidency.*
Maldwyn A. Jones is Commonwealth Fund Professor of American History at the University of London. He has been a visiting professor at Harvard and at the universities of Chicago and Pennsylvania. Professor Jones has written extensively on American ethnic groups and is the author of *American Immigration,* a volume in the *Chicago History of American Civilization.*

Library of Congress Catalog Card No: 73-8423
© 1976 Grolier Enterprises Inc
Printed in USA
ISBN-0-7172-8113-2

**The Danbury Press**
A Division of Grolier Enterprises Inc
PUBLISHER: Robert B. Clarke
EDITORIAL DIRECTOR: Wallace S. Murray
ADVISORY EDITORS: Edward Humphrey, Bernard S. Cayne, John S. Cox, Alan H. Smith, Hallberg Hallmundsson, Donald R. Young, Robert L. Hurtgen, Eric E. Akerman, Frank H. Senyk

**Orbis Publishing Ltd**
EDITORIAL DIRECTORS: Martin Heller, Brian Innes
MANAGING EDITOR: Edward Horton
DEPUTY EDITOR: Lawson Nagel
DESIGNER: Grant Gibson
PICTURE EDITOR: Lynda Poley

**Contributors to this volume include:**
I. H. Bartlett, Carnegie-Mellon University, and Virginia Bartlett; H. S. Commager; Marcus Cunliffe; Michael Heale, University of Lancaster; W. S. Hudson, University of Rochester; M. A. Jones; James Potter, London School of Economics.

# Introduction

This volume deals with American life and thought between 1815 and 1860. The era could be seen as a peaceful interval between the end of one war and the beginning of another. But it was emphatically not an inert period. There was hectic activity out West, to which Volume 5 is devoted. Nor was conflict entirely absent. Apart from city riots, lawlessness in some frontier zones, and Indian wars, there was the tension of sectional antagonism which was to polarize so many aspects of American existence—the theme of Volume 6.

This volume discusses the release of national energies in other fields. Here is a portrait of a people on the move, and at work, at innumerable tasks—most of which seemed urgent, and sometimes glorious. Among the writers who tried to catch its essence were Ralph Waldo Emerson and Walt Whitman. The two men differed in many ways. Emerson the New Englander graduated from Harvard and for a few years served as a Unitarian minister. Whitman, a "rough" by his own confession (or boast), was largely self-educated and earned a living as a carpenter as well as a journalist. Yet they had several features in common. Both were worried by certain tendencies—above all a kind of lack of inner strength.

But, perhaps paradoxically, they recommended and celebrated the very qualities that now and then disturbed them. Their own writings were deliberately loose in form, because they were in search of new forms. They urged their fellow-Americans to forget Europe, to ignore rote-learning, to strike out as individuals. "Individualism" was a new word in the language, used by the French traveler Alexis de Tocqueville to describe the provisional, questing, irreverent mood of the American people. In his essays Emerson told his contemporaries to think of themselves as advance scouts for modern man. In poems such as "Song of Myself," Whitman evoked the flux, the exuberance, the sheer variety of existence in America.

In their search for the American character, both measured the nation's material achievements against the high standards set by the Founding Fathers. Being themselves individualists, even in a way loners, they were less impressed than some of their fellow countrymen by the spread and bustle of organized institutions. They did not care much for committees, or political parties; they were democrats rather than Democrats, Emerson more reticently so than Whitman. Whitman once spoke of himself of being "both in and out of the game." Yet though neither was exactly a typical American, they did typify their nation.

Thus Emerson exemplified the moral earnestness of the Puritan tradition. New England was one of the strongholds of education and religion. Vigorous in trade and commerce, it also sent out teachers and preachers across the land. Though not himself a reformer, Emerson was in touch with most of the reform movements of the day. And his message—for instance in such slogans as "Hitch your wagon to a star"—was easily interpreted as encouragement for the pioneer settler or businessman.

Whitman, too, expressed the numerous and shifting currents of American life and thought. Among his early publications was a temperance novel, about the evils of drink. Though he never attended college he was at one stage a schoolteacher; and he would have counted education as one of the precious elements of American democracy. A Quaker by upbringing, he had a deep though unorthodox religious instinct. And while he ceased to be a partisan Democrat when he abandoned journalism for poetry, Whitman sensed the importance of politics. Political oratory was a popular entertainment with deeper undertones—a theater of the street. Political action allowed the crowd of common men to express their individual preferences, and then to discover their collective identity in the will of the majority

In other words, Emerson and Whitman were, in their respective fashions, American patriots. One of the figures who fascinated them was Andrew Jackson. A brother of Whitman's was named after Jackson (two others were named George Washington Whitman and Benjamin Franklin Whitman). True, Jackson was a little too much associated with warfare to suit reformers who wanted to abolish war. The fact that he was a slaveholder bothered some people. Indeed, it was not only the wealthy who voted against Jackson. But where Emerson and Whitman expressed the age, Jackson represented it. Even his enemies sensed that "Andy" was a hero for the common man; and that the American character was being built around the idea of the common man.

# COMMERCIAL
# MAIL STAGE,
### ☞ IN THIRTY-NINE HOURS,
## From Boston to New York,
### ☞ *CARRYING ONLY SIX PASSENGERS.*

## Runs by the way of Worcester, Stafford Springs,
**Hartford, Middletown, New-Haven to New-York....Leaves Boston every day at 1 o'clock,
P. M.---arrives at Hartford at 7 o'clock, A M.---arrives at New-Haven 3 o'clock P. M.---
arrives at New-York, 6 o'clock, A. M.**

## *Returning.......Leaves New-York for Boston*
every day at half past seven o'clock, A. M.---leaves New-Haven at 10 o'clock, P. M.---leaves
Hartford half past 5 o'clock, A. M.---arrives at **Boston** half past 11 o'clock, P. M.---making
*Thirty-nine hours*, it being seven hours sooner than ever performed before.

*The Proprietors solicit the Patronage of the Public, and pledge themselves that every exer*
tion shall be made for their accommodation.

**Fare to be paid in Boston, New Haven and New York.**

☞ **For Seats apply at the Stage Office, Exchange Coffee-House, entrance in Con-**
gress-Street—Boston.—Col. Reuben Sikes, Worcester.—Bennett's Coffee-House, Hartford,—Butler's Hotel, New-Haven,—Courtland-Street,
No. 1, New-York.

☞ **For Seats in the *Accommodation Stages*, apply as above.**

**BOSTON,** *February,* 1815.

ROWE & HOOPER, PRINTERS, 78, STATE-STREET—BOSTON.

# Contents

*Chapter I*

# A DISTINCTIVE SOCIETY

*"The great advantage of the Americans," wrote the penetrating French observer Alexis de Tocqueville, "is . . . that they are born equal instead of becoming so." But this was not their only distinctive quality. Nevertheless it was apparent to all visitors that the American people—for better or for worse —had taken on a shape of their own. Some saw them as lovers of simplicity, while others thought they hankered after wealth; to some, America was a classless society, but to others it had clearly defined social divisions. There were many sides to the American character, but it had a style all its own.*

# The Democratic Style

By the early nineteenth century, the American character seemed to be more or less formed. Americans and foreigners alike noted the same features, and their comments did not vary much between 1815 and 1860. Indeed, much of what they said could still serve as a description of American character in the twentieth century.

Nearly all, for instance, took for granted that there were regional differences within the overall American type. The New Englander was often portrayed as a quintessential Yankee, puritanical in outlook, and a hard, shrewd bargainer. The white southerner tended to be represented as a plantation owner: impulsive, hospitable, brave to the edge of folly, and usually not a good businessman. The farmer of the Middle West was hailed as a sturdy, resourceful pioneer. The actual pioneer on the fringes of settlement came in for less praise than in later accounts. In the first decades of the century, he was frequently described as a misfit, in danger of slipping back into savagery. On the whole, though, the regional stereotypes were set. So for that matter were the racial ones. Negro slaves were variously and somewhat inconsistently depicted as lazy, carefree, cunning, harmless, or dangerous.

Putting the whole picture together, there was agreement that an American was almost instantly recognizable in appearance, speech, and behavior. The average Englishman, it was said, looked like the John Bull drawn in cartoons. He was red-faced, thickset, and hearty, with an air of self-importance. The average American of the period, to judge from travelers' accounts, resembled the Uncle Sam who was beginning to replace Brother Jonathan as the cartoonist's symbol for the United States. He was lean and craggy in build, with a bony face and a pale complexion. In temperament he was reserved, determined, sober. Some observers found him humorless, and apt to drink too much without becoming cheerful in the process. Nearly every foreigner testified that Americans were hardworking, except for small batches of "clay-eaters" and others who suffered from poor diet, swamp fever, and similar misfortunes. These were found mostly in the back country, and especially in low-lying parts of the Mississippi Valley. Otherwise, the American impressed outsiders as vigorous and independent.

Whether these traits were thought likeable depended on the temperament of the observer. Richard Cobbett, himself a vigorous and independent Englishman writing in the second decade of the century, gave the American high marks. The farmers (who particularly interested him) were, Cobbett said, confident without being conceited. They were, in contrast with middle-class Englishmen, straightforward and generous. Such tributes remind us that words like "self-made" and "go-ahead" were American coinages of the Jacksonian era—new expressions to describe new attitudes.

The novelty lay not in mere energy. Plenty of Europeans, after all, were busy, enterprising people. What Cobbett and others found fresh in the American situation was the relative classlessness of the society. True, Americans worried about *status*. Foreign travelers poked fun at them for calling one another "Judge," "Doctor," "Reverend," "Colonel," and so on—when these designations might not really have been earned. In Charles Dickens's novel *Martin Chuzzlewit* (1843–44) the hero found he was sharing a New York boardinghouse with "four majors . . . , two colonels, one general, and a captain." He "could not help thinking how strongly officered the American militia must be; and wondering . . . whether the officers commanded each other; or if they did not, where on earth the privates came from." But these, after all, were only personal titles, so widespread as to be comic. There were as yet no powerful families with big estates. There was no hereditary aristocracy. At one end of the social scale were some fairly affluent people, genteel in conduct and with a certain amount of family pride. At the bottom end of the scale were some native-born Americans and some immigrants, living with a simplicity that approached squalor. The great middle mass, however, was neither rich nor poor. Students of this unique middleness, including the American writer James Fenimore Cooper, sometimes called it "mediocrity." Usually they meant not that Americans were mediocre in the modern sense of being talentless, but that uniformity of condition revealed the happy medium between the undesirable extremes of opulence and poverty.

Such a scene appalled some European visitors, and worried fastidious Americans. Félix de Beaujour, a French contemporary of Cobbett, emphasized the money-minded bleakness of the new nation. In his book, translated into English in 1814, Beaujour said:

> Virtue has always been considered as the principle, or the chief spring of all republics; but that of the American republic seems to be an unbounded love of money. This is the effect of the political equality that reigns there, and which leaves to the citizen no other distinction than that of riches, and invites them to fill their coffers by every means in their power. Every thing among them favours this vile cupidity; their disdain for the agreeable arts, . . . their coarse intemperance, which deprive them of all love and activity for every thing that is not personal. . . . With them, justice is the result of calculation, but never of sentiment. She is deaf to the cries of the wretched, and particularly of the foreigner; and in the greatest part of their commercial towns . . . , it is the shortest as well as the surest road to arrive at a fortune.

Beaujour's views were echoed by other travelers. The

*For all its supposed classlessness American society was far from egalitarian. Left: A woodcut from a New York paper (February 1860) shows an impoverished gathering huddled round a fire. Below: The men in Henry Sargent's The Dinner Party enjoy a bounteous spread.*

Scottish army captain Thomas Hamilton (*Men and Manners in America*, 1833) reported of the American: "Mammon is his god, he prays to him, not merely with his lips, but with all the force of his body and mind." A few years later Dickens claimed that Americans worshiped the "Almighty Dollar."

Another common observation was the amazing amount of freedom given to American children. This surprised, and generally shocked, Europeans even before 1800. They went on mentioning it all through the nineteenth century. Harriet Martineau, a sympathetic English visitor, felt that "the children of Americans have the advantage of the best possible early discipline; that of activity and self-dependence." The English novelist Anthony Trollope, who came to the United States on the eve of the Civil War, did not agree: "I must protest that American babies are an unhappy race. They eat and drink as they please; they are never punished; they are never banished, snubbed, and kept in the background as children are kept with us." In a burlesque Fourth of July oration of 1856, the American humorist "John H. Phoenix" (Captain George Horatio Derby) tells a story that bears out these impressions:

A parsimonious merchant . . . in Boston, kept his counting-room open on Independence Day, where he sat with his clerk, a boy of ten or twelve years of age, busy over his accounts, while the noise and uproar of the celebration were resounding without. Looking up from his employment, he perceived the unfortunate youth, perched upon his high stool, engaged in picking his nose, a practice that the merchant had frequently . . . taken him to task for.

"William," he exclaimed, "why will you persist in that dirty practice? I am astonished at you."

"I don't care," whimpered the unhappy boy. "It's Independence Day, and it's my nose, and I'll pick thunder out of it."

## Individualism and Conformity

One other feature tended to be noticed, and deplored, by American as well as European commentators. This was the role played by public opinion. Since there was no royal court or aristocracy in the United States, there was no group at the top to set a standard of behavior. In theory, there was almost infinite scope for each individual to do as he pleased. In practice, however, American conduct was policed by public opinion. Anxious to win approval from their neighbors, middling Americans seemed excessively willing to conform to social pressures. Here was a paradox. The French political thinker Alexis de Tocque-

*Boys and girls romp gaily in this watercolor (c.1815). European visitors commented on the freedom allowed American children.*

ville surveyed the American scene in the 1830s, and said: "In most of the operations of the mind each American appeals only to the individual effort of his own understanding." The very word "individualism" first came into English from Tocqueville's book, to convey the uniquely self-involved outlook of the American. But Tocqueville also said: "What strikes me is that the immense majority of spirits join together in certain *common opinions*." He tried to resolve the paradox by suggesting there was a dual tendency in American life—one tendency "leading the mind of every man to untried thoughts, the other prohibiting him from thinking at all."

It is clear that Tocqueville was not just inventing notions about America. We can back up his remarks by citing two others from a host of witnesses, both of them also referring to the 1830s. One was the Austrian immigrant Francis Grund:

> The habit of conforming to each others' opinions, and the penalty set upon every transgression of that kind, are sufficient to prevent a man from wearing a coat cut in a different fashion, or a shirt collar no longer *à la mode*, or, in fact, to do, or say, or appear anything which could render him unpopular. . . . In no other place, I believe, is there such a stress laid upon "saving appearances."

The other witness is James Fenimore Cooper, an upright, crusty man who loved his country but sometimes found it hard to like. "They say!"—this, he exploded, was the invisible tyrant in the United States. People went in fear of the mysterious force of public opinion. In some respects Americans were boldly individualistic. In others, especially where ideas were concerned, they were timid. Among the worst culprits, according to Cooper, were political demagogues who flattered the ignorant into thinking they knew best, and newspaper editors, who specialized in hypocrisy and slander. It was "often made a matter of boasting," said Cooper, that the United States contained so many newspapers. "It were wiser to make it a cause of mourning, since the quality, in this instance, diminishes in an inverse ratio to the quantity." In America,

> Whoever opposes the interests, or wishes of the public, however right in principle, or justifiable by circumstances, finds little sympathy; for, in a democracy, resisting the wishes of the many, is resisting the sovereign, in his caprices.

More sanguine patriots, while they might admit that the "tyranny of the majority" was a regrettable feature of American life, felt it was a small price to pay for all that had been gained. If the alternative was rule by an elite minority, they far preferred what they had got.

The American character, to recapitulate, seemed to have taken fairly definite shape by the early nineteenth century. The history of the United States up to the Civil War is largely the working out of the ideology within which this character operated. Tocqueville, the most brilliant inter-

*Alexis de Tocqueville left France in 1831 to study American prisons. His interest in practical democracy led to remarkably astute observations of American people and institutions.*

Service de Documentation de la Reunion des Musées Nationaux

preter of the democratic psyche, saw that Americans needed no coercion from public opinion to subscribe to the basic rules of the society. "The great majority," he perceived, "understand republican principles in the most democratic sense. . . . It is an opinion so general and so little disputed . . . that one might almost call it a faith."

## The Nation's Democratic Creed

What were the ground rules of the American democratic faith—bearing in mind of course that they were confined mainly to white male Americans? We shall not find them set out in any formal manifesto or treatise during the years 1815–60. There was remarkably little exploration of the democratic creed by American intellectuals. The reason probably is that the ideology was so pervasive —except in the South, and even there, *white* society was (by European standards) democratic. Since democratic federal republicanism went unchallenged, and since America was so evidently prospering, the ideology was taken for granted. Ritual gestures were made to it, notably amid the speeches and firework displays of Independence Day. But on each Fourth of July the oratory simply restated—possibly for hours on end—the creed as enshrined in the Declaration of Independence and the Constitution.

John H. Phoenix supplies a parody of a typical address:

In this great and desirable country, any man may become rich, provided he will make money; and any man may be educated, if he will learn, and has money to pay for his board and schooling; and any man may become great, and of weight in the community, if he will take care of his health, and eat sufficiently. . . .

Moreover, I assert it unblushingly, any man in this country may marry any woman he pleases—the only difficulty being for him to find any woman that he does please.

A significant detail in the creed was the idea that even the highest office in the land lay open to competition. In Phoenix's words:

I do not wish to flatter this audience; I do not intend to be thought particularly complimentary; but I do assure you that there is not a man present who, if he had votes enough, might not be elected President. And this important fact is the result not so much of any particular merit or virtue on your part, as of the nature of our glorious, liberal, republican institutions.

Despite the facetiousness of these passages, Phoenix quite accurately caught the tone of this annual ceremony. In effect, it reassured every American male that the future lay open to him. His democratic legacy was like a skeleton key that could unlock every door. His own responsibility was to find the doors and to pass through as many of them as possible.

Or, to change the figure, American life resembled a footrace in which everyone must compete or suffer failure and humiliation. The democratic faith blended competition and equality. Competition meant zeal and hard work. Logically, if there were winners there must also be losers. The creed emphasized winning. A skeptic might argue that a young man aiming at the presidency had only one chance in many thousands of attaining his object. A believer would respond that the youngster had as good a chance as anyone else. Nor was this equivalent to a lottery, in which the luck of the draw determined the outcome. In competition for the presidency, an ambitious person could summon up all his latent gifts of ingenuity, integrity, eloquence, and sheer will. Ralph Waldo Emerson spoke of this reservoir of democratic individualism as the "unsearched might of man." Again, Americans such as the economist Mathew Carey were much readier than Europeans to insist that there was practically no limit to the number of winners. The wealth of the community was not a finite amount, in which one

*Conviviality and patriotism pervade Susan Merrett's* Picnic Scene – Fourth of July, *set in Weymouth, Massachusetts. The spirit depicted here prevailed throughout the country.*

Courtesy of the Art Institute of Chicago

man's gain was another man's loss. On the contrary, it increased through the sum of individual efforts. As the country grew it must infallibly become wealthier. Even a selfish person, amassing money and possessions, could not help but add to the total wealth, and benefit others through his own transactions.

## Free Competition for All

On the equality side of the creed, society's duty was to ensure that each competitor started off on a par with his fellows. There must be no handicaps or cheating in the race. Wherever feasible, obstacles must be removed from the course. When these conditions had been met, it would be every man for himself; neither the government nor any other agency ought to intervene to help either the strong or the weak. Corruption must be avoided. Individual initiative must not be sapped. Men pointed to the Indians as examples of what befell people who lacked the instinct of private enterprise. Their tribes were collapsing in face of the white advance. Their warriors, once they were living off annuities as wards of the government, degenerated into drunken, disease-ridden torpor. The Jeffersonian and Jacksonian faith, as it triumphed in America, maintained that the best government was that which governed least. It should referee the race, and nothing more. "Its true strength," said Andrew Jackson in 1832,

> consists in leaving individuals and States as much as possible to themselves; in making itself felt, not in its power, but in its beneficence; not in its control, but in its protection; not in binding the States more closely to the center, but leaving each to move unobstructed in its proper orbit.

In his essay on *Civil Disobedience* (1849), Henry David Thoreau, the rebel of Massachusetts, said much the same thing, though from a very different perspective:

> Government is at best but an expedient. . . . *It* does not keep the country free. *It* does not settle the West. *It* does not educate. The character inherent in the American people has done all that has been accomplished; and it would have done somewhat more, if the government had not sometimes got in its way.

One might reply that the vision of minimal government did not altogether fit the facts of Jacksonian America. The activities of the United States regular army did a good deal to open up and civilize the West, through exploration, surveying, road building, peace-keeping, and the like. More obviously, the federal government aided various branches of American industry and commerce by means of protective tariffs which sheltered native products from foreign competition. The businessmen who profited from these policies did not protest that their initiative was being sapped. At state level, governmental activity was correspondingly greater, and again not contested on grounds of principle.

Such anomalies would have presented no difficulty for an American spokesman of the era. The function of the tariff, he could have noted, was protection, not control. He could have explained, quite correctly, that government activity at federal and at state level was aimed at creating or guaranteeing the conditions for the freest (and therefore best) operation of the system of individual enterprise. The two levels of government, for instance, had immense areas of public land to dispose of. There was much debate over exactly how it should be disposed. But there was virtually no dispute over the proposition that it should be turned over, as quickly and cheaply as possible, to private ownership. In the same way, legislation and court rulings were in essence directed at maximizing the opportunities for private enterprise. A celebrated example is the *Charles River Bridge* case, decided by the Supreme Court in 1837. This was a toll bridge linking Boston and Cambridge, Massachusetts. The owners of the bridge company brought suit against Massachusetts for chartering another bridge nearby, which was eventually to become public property. The company argued that the new bridge impaired its own rights. Chief Justice Roger B. Taney, speaking for the Court, ruled against the Charles River Bridge Company. His decision seemed to weaken the sanctity of contracts which had been so marked a feature of the Court under Chief Justice John Marshall. In truth, the fundamental concern of American authorities was to safeguard the economic well-being of the society. Sometimes this led them to do things, sometimes to refrain from doing things. There was less and less support for the concept of government as an institution endowed with a permanent, positive role.

## The Land of Opportunity

What Thoreau dubbed "the character inherent in the American people" thus connoted a balancing of competition and egalitarianism. The ground rules of the democratic faith endeavored to bring these together, in the shape of *equality of opportunity*. Given such equality, America was bound to flourish. Without it, the nation might perish.

This equality was envisaged in three main forms: political, economic, and educational. Each was designed to enable men to compete on fair terms. Political equality of opportunity meant, first, that every male adult American should be entitled to vote, in local, state, and national elections. This had not been attempted in the colonial era. But in the first decades of independence, property requirements were steadily whittled away. By the middle of the nineteenth century, practically everywhere in the United States, a white male reaching the age of twenty-one could vote in all the elections that affected him. He could also now stand for almost any office in the land. In a few states, free black citizens were also entitled to vote. The immigrant, too, could quickly qualify. A law reenacted in 1802 allowed immigrants to claim full American citizenship after five years of residence. Legally or illegally, many immigrants—at any rate in local and state elections—were lured to the polls long before the five years were up. The sole disqualification was that, under the Constitution, the presidency was confined to native-born citizens.

Ideologically, a key aspect of equality of political opportunity was "rotation." This had been much discussed in the period of revolutionary constitution-making. It continued to figure prominently in Jeffersonian and Jacksonian America, as a crucial condition of political health. As a constitutional mechanism, it restricted elected

*Andrew Jackson was a product of the frontier. By winning the highest office in the land, he proved that political success was not confined to the well-bred.*

The Metropolitan Museum of Art, Harris Brisbane Dick Fund, 1964 (detail)

officials such as state governors to a limited period in office, and then barred them from succeeding themselves. The idea was to prevent the emergence of a semihereditary ruling clique. Another idea was that men in power ought to return frequently to "the bosom of the people," so as to renew contact with the mass of citizens and to be freshly recruited from them. Hence, too, the necessity for frequent elections.

In Jackson's presidency, "rotation in office" became a fighting issue. His opponents accused him of having perverted the democratic faith. He contended that the victorious party in an election ought to be at liberty to replace officeholders in order to preserve rotation. His enemies said that he was introducing the "spoils system" ("to the victors belong the spoils"), by making party loyalty the criterion for securing a postmastership, a place in a customhouse, or some other snug berth. Undoubtedly the Jackson men did have a political motive. Their followers were more likely to exert themselves, and keep in line, if there was the prospect of a reward. But there is no reason to suppose that Jackson was insincere. Jefferson before him had thought in the same way. Jackson was expressing a basic item in the American creed when he proposed—unavailingly—in 1829 that all federal offices should be limited to a four-year period:

> In a country where offices are created solely for the benefit of the people no one man has any more intrinsic right to official station than another. . . . No individual wrong is, therefore, done by removal, since neither appointment to nor continuance in office is matter of right. . . . It is the People, and they alone, who have a right to complain when a bad officer is substituted for a good one. He who is removed has the same means of obtaining a living that are employed by the millions who never held office.

In the same message, Jackson declared that "the duties of all public officers are, or at least admit of being made, so plain and simple that men of intelligence may readily qualify themselves for their performance." He himself, after all, had been a planter, a lawyer, a member of Congress, a judge, and a soldier, with very little previous training. Though Jackson was reelected for a second term in 1832, he was doubtless sincere, too, in having previously recommended to Congress a constitutional amendment limiting the presidency to one four-year term—a restriction Jefferson had also favored. In the event, both followed the precedent set by George Washington, of retiring from office after eight years. This was a voluntary recognition that the presidency ought not to be exempt from the same general principle of rotation.

The second vital form was equality of economic opportunity. The *Charles River Bridge* case falls under this heading. Monopoly—the capacity of an individual or a group to control some economic lifeline—was spoken of with horror. Its offense was not in enabling some people to enrich themselves, but in necessarily preventing others from doing the same. The Charles River Bridge proprietors had long enjoyed a virtual monopoly of tolls. Nobody objected until the issue suddenly came alive. The proprietors then appeared as a bunch of selfish capitalists who were seeking to hinder the free expansion of economic life in the Boston area.

Monopoly was a deadly sin against the democratic faith. It was a highly emotive word, implying both unfair advantage seized by unscrupulous men, and a device that threatened the nation's economic health. In the pre-Civil War era, before the arrival of the giant corporations, the charge of monopoly was most often leveled against banks. The Bank of the United States was a special target. According to President Jackson, it dominated the nation's financial structure. The manipulation of currency was a secret realm, open to the rich but not the "humble members of society—the farmers, mechanics, and laborers." Worse still, control of the bank was partly in the hands of foreign stockholders, who were in a position to undermine the citadel of American democracy. Whether Jackson's charges were justified is another question. The relevant point is that he made them in the classic vocabulary of Americanism, and defeated his critics by standing on this unassailable terrain.

The third main element was equality of educational opportunity. Sooner or later, every prominent American declared his attachment to the principle of free universal schooling. In practice, this ideal was not attained throughout the Union before 1860. More money was put into private schools and colleges. Nevertheless, the creed called for a high degree of literacy. The idea is neatly expressed in a Pennsylvania announcement of 1784: "The spirit and character of a republic is very different from that of a monarchy, and can only be imbibed by education." Or as the Northwest Ordinance put it: "Religion, morality, and knowledge, being necessary to good government, and the happiness of mankind, schools and the means of education shall forever be encouraged." To Jefferson, access to the educational ladder would furnish the country with a "natural aristocracy" to replace the "artificial" aristocracy with which Europe was burdened. Common schooling would put all American children on the same footing. It would imbue them with patriotism and religious feeling. So said many a speech. Educators like Horace Mann of Massachusetts claimed not only that education would enable young Americans to play a part in political decisions, as voters and perhaps legislators and officeholders, but also be indispensable as an economic weapon. An educated people, Mann contended, could not be a poor people; knowledge and prosperity were inseparable. Education was, in short, presented as a great, essential panacea. With it, America was certain to flourish. Without it, the nation was likely to founder.

## Inheritance and the Democratic Faith

Were these three preconditions sufficient? John H. Phoenix sounded cynical when he proclaimed, tongue-in-cheek, that any man might do well if he either made money or had money to start with. The metaphor of a race is appealing when it applies to the start. We can respond to the image of eager contestants, toes touching the same line, and the government as a benevolent referee with a starting-pistol raised aloft. What though if the competitors were *not* equally placed at the outset? And what of the later stages of the race: would not some of the runners be too far ahead to be overtaken, and then confer an unfair benefit, through the privileges of wealth, upon their children?

Americans were well aware of the potential risks. They insisted that the three types of equality of opportunity must be achieved, and must be treated as a single, joint democratic prerequisite. In addition, they considered other features. They occasionally worried about inherited wealth. Self-madeness was excellent. Unearned money offended against the principles of individual democratic enterprise. Also it was thought bad for the inheritors. If an Indian was ruined by a small dole from the government, a young American who came into money from his family was surely in no less danger of losing his moral fiber. Some radicals toyed with the theory that no one should be permitted to inherit wealth. This would have sustained the image of the fairly competitive race. But it clashed with the equally powerful American belief that private property was sacred. In an era when there were no federal income taxes or death duties, the proposal to confiscate property on a person's death was unthinkable.

In obedience to the tenets ingrained in the American character, men hit upon answers that satisfied them. For one thing, there was such abundance of economic opportunity—jobs, land, trade, manufacture—that nobody need feel the pinch. For another thing, nobody as yet was inordinately richer than his fellows. The American way, they reiterated, was a modest one; this was a "middling" people. Thirdly, if some men did become quite rich, they could put their money back into the community in the form of philanthropy. And a favorite form of giving was for education, which strengthened equality of opportunity for others. Finally, it was assumed that something in the nature of American life automatically prevented families from transmitting their possessions from generation to generation—"easy come, easy go"; "shirtsleeves to shirtsleeves in three generations." The American character and the American democratic faith subtly interacted to produce the sort of person who unmistakably disclosed himself, in any of the four corners of the earth, to be a representative of Uncle Sam.

# Chapter 2

# THE ERA OF THE COMMON MAN

*"No sooner do you set foot upon American ground," wrote Tocqueville, "than you are stunned by a kind of tumult; a confused clamor is heard on every side, and a thousand simultaneous voices demand the satisfaction of their social wants." The nation's first six presidents had been gentlemen from Virginia and Massachusetts, but by the 1820s the expanding frontier had given rise to a strengthening of the democratic spirit in American life. As the land was opened up, so the political process was made more accessible. A new party system arose to meet new circumstances and the choice of the people was more directly felt in the election of leaders.*

# Politics in Jackson's America

The character of the American people has been expressed more fully in their politics than in any other activity. This was particularly true of the period between 1815 and 1860. In literature and the arts, Americans continued to chafe under the dominance of Europe. In politics, however, they boasted to a skeptical world that they were the creators of a new form of government which enabled men to live together in dignity, freedom, and harmony.

Politics, too, was one of the most popular of American activities in this period. Foreign visitors commented on the passion for talking politics—in hotels and bars, on steamboats and stagecoaches, wherever men gathered together. By the 1840s, about 80 per cent of the electorate was going to the polls in presidential elections—a proportion never equalled in the twentieth century.

The purpose of the American political system, many believed, was not merely to allow Americans to live harmoniously together, but also to set an enlightened example to other peoples. When Andrew Jackson left the White House in 1837 after two terms as president, he shared with his fellow citizens his thoughts on the destiny of their country: "Providence . . . has chosen you as the guardians of freedom to preserve it for the benefit of the human race." Jackson and his contemporaries were highly conscious of their special obligations to their country and to mankind. The men of the Revolution had bequeathed to them a form of government which departed daringly from those in Europe, one which depended on the consent of the governed. Even after half a century, the experiment in republicanism could still evoke a certain awe among Americans. They believed that they had all but perfected a unique form of government which enabled men to enjoy—and to exhibit—the blessings of freedom.

By the age of Jackson, most white men enjoyed the

*The new era called for new modes of political expression. Above: "The Grand Fantastical Parade" parodies a New York street demonstration in 1833. Left: In George Caleb Bingham's painting an earnest candidate woos potential supporters.*

right to vote. They increasingly exercised this right. Politicians became highly conscious of the power of the electorate, which they wooed with all the resources at their command. They abandoned the patrician style of an earlier generation in favor of one with the common touch. One state governor fortified his plebeian image by spitting eighty-two times in the course of his inaugural address— a practice which (mercifully) did not become expected of all political aspirants. National party conventions, massive open-air rallies, lengthy and festive torchlight processions, all became part of the new kind of politics.

The men who assumed the leadership of the nation's affairs after 1815 were very conscious that they were a new generation. In the early years of the Republic, the country had been guided by men who had been tested in the fires of the Revolution, men who had actually helped to create America's free institutions. As the veterans of the Revolution passed away, Americans became uneasily aware that their experiment in republicanism was passing into new and untried hands. During the presidential election of 1824, for example, newspapers throughout the country drew attention to the fact that, for the first time, the White House would be occupied by someone who was not a Founding Father. The candidates themselves tried to stress their links with the revolutionary past. Andrew Jackson's partisans reminded the electorate that Jackson had served briefly in the War of Independence as a boy soldier—and (even more glorious) he had actually been wounded! "Did his claim to the gratitude of his country rest here," wrote his campaign biographer with stunning boldness, "it would be enough." The shedding of blood in the cause of freedom, it seemed, qualified Jackson for the presidency. That such a breathtaking demand could be made, even in the heat of an election campaign, is a mark of the increasing difficulty of identifying the nation's leading men with the Revolution.

Jackson's supporters could make a tenuous claim for their candidate as a revolutionary hero, but he was the last of whom this could be said. When Martin Van Buren entered the White House in 1837, he hesitantly reminded his fellow citizens that he was the first president not to

*Andrew Jackson's victory over the British at New Orleans in 1815 made him a national hero. This, combined with his humble origins, gave Jackson an attractive political image.*

have been born before the Revolution. It was as if he was afraid that Providence would smile less warmly on one not touched by the magic of that era. The duty of carrying forward America's unique experiment in liberty and self-government had now fallen on men who had grown up since the War of Independence. The trust was an awesome one.

The emergence of a new political leadership had, of course, been taking place for some years. The War of 1812, in particular, introduced a number of fresh faces to the political stage. The war had been brought about in part by the efforts of a young group of politicians known as the War Hawks, and it had been fought by soldiers whose service in the revolutionary conflict had been slight or nonexistent. Several of those who thus rose to prominence continued to hold dominating positions in American politics until the 1850s. One reason why the warriors of 1812 were to prove acceptable as political leaders was that the conflict enabled them to present

Courtesy of the New-York Historical Society (detail)

National Portrait Gallery, Washington (detail)

National Portrait Gallery, Washington (detail)

themselves as defenders of American republicanism. The war gave the new generation a priceless opportunity to defy and to humiliate the same enemy that their fathers had fought, an opportunity to demonstrate their own dedication to the great American experiment. As if to emphasize that the war was but another act in the revolutionary drama, it soon became known to Americans as the Second War of Independence. To a degree, the War of 1812 was to the second generation what the revolutionary war had been to the first: it proved that they were Americans. Participation in it was an incomparable political asset in the Jacksonian era. Every presidential election from 1824 to 1852 featured among the principal contenders (for either the presidency or the vice-presidency) at least one hero of that war.

One of the most eloquent figures to emerge in these years was Henry Clay of Kentucky. Elected Speaker of the House of Representatives in 1811, he first achieved prominence as a belligerent advocate of the nation's rights during the events preceding the war. Quick-witted, articulate, impulsive, and popular, in the decades after 1815 Clay was the most accomplished congressional leader of his generation. He moved less certainly in a larger arena. Ever fond of a wager, Clay, as one colleague noted, retained the gambler's temperament in political life. All too often, he played and lost. But the nationalism that he had revealed during the War of 1812 always remained with him. Believing that the key to national strength and unity was economic development, he elaborated his "American System." The central feature of this was a protective tariff to encourage the growth of industry, thus creating a domestic market in which

*From left: Political giants Henry Clay, John C. Calhoun, and Daniel Webster. Though they were the most influential spokesmen of their time, none managed to achieve the highest political office in the land.*

American farmers could sell their products. The tariff would also produce revenue which could be spent on "internal improvements," generally transportation projects. This program implied a loose construction of the Constitution and a fairly vigorous role for the federal government. It was thus regarded with suspicion by southerners sensitive to states' rights. But despite lapses, Clay continued to champion some variation of his American System through the rest of his life.

As a westerner, Clay could embrace a philosophy of positive government more readily than politicians from some other areas. His constituents tended to favor federal aid for internal improvements (thus making eastern markets more accessible) and tariff protection for certain products. He also escaped close identification with either North or South and could readily present himself as a national patriot. Thus, Clay was able to offer his services as a negotiator during the great sectional disputes that periodically threatened to disrupt the Union, earning the title "the Great Conciliator." Political ambition as well as patriotism moved Clay to action. He gambled for the highest stakes by repeatedly throwing himself into races for the presidency, but he never won the coveted prize.

Another who first rose to prominence as a War Hawk was John C. Calhoun of South Carolina. Later, he served in President Monroe's cabinet as secretary of war, introducing certain army reforms and advocating a vigorous federal road-building program. In these years, Calhoun was regarded as one of the most nationalistic of America's public men. In the early 1820s, when he eyed the presidency, he was one of the few candidates who could expect significant support in both North and South. Calhoun was an intellectual who prided himself on being a man of action, and his powerful mind and bold stands made him one of the political giants of the day. His acquaintances testified to his charm, though one observer immortalized him as "the cast iron man who looks as if he had never been born."

While Clay and Calhoun first displayed their talents in Congress, Andrew Jackson displayed his on the battlefield. His dramatic victory over a larger British force at New Orleans in 1815 made him the most celebrated figure of his day. His popularity remained with him, making him one of the most successful vote-winners in American history. His appeal rested in part on his fame as the Hero of New Orleans, and in part on what he symbolized. Orphaned early in life, Jackson was the quintessential self-made man—a lawyer, planter, and soldier who had hacked his way from obscurity to prominence. Making his career in the western state of Tennessee, he seemed to personify many of the qualities of the frontier. He possessed a simple and direct manner, an iron will, a natural wisdom which came from reading men rather than books, and a refusal to recognize any man as his better. Jackson, in short, seemed very much a product of the New World, a living proof that in the United States, courage and determination counted for more than birth and education. On his election to the presidency in 1828, he assumed leadership of what was to become the Democratic party, helping to make possible its image as the party of the common man.

A number of other warriors of 1812 were also helped on their way to high political office by their success on the battlefield. General William Henry Harrison, whose reputation rested on modest victories over the Indians and the British on the western frontier, was to be elected president in 1840. One of his fellow officers in the West had been Colonel Richard M. Johnson, who won fame as the reputed slayer of the great Indian chief Tecumseh. Johnson received his reward in 1837 when he became vice president of the United States. But not all the leading men of the era had been associated with the War of 1812; the most notable exceptions were Martin Van Buren and Daniel Webster. Significantly, both came from the Northeast where the second war with Britain had not been particularly popular.

Daniel Webster was a phenomenon. Dubbed "the God-like Daniel" for his formidable looks and his magnificent voice, it was said by his friends that he was living proof that man was made in the image of God. A brilliant constitutional lawyer and a superb orator, Webster joined Clay and Calhoun as one of the great "triumvirate" in the Senate who passed judgment on the issues of the day. A strong nationalist, Webster established himself as a champion of the sanctity of the Union. But while he was admired in New England and even revered in his own state of Massachusetts, Webster held little appeal outside his own section. This was in part because he had been a Federalist in his first years in politics. He had not participated in the near-treasonable proceedings of the Hartford Convention in 1814, when New England Federalists had discussed seceding from the Union. But his early membership of that apparently unpatriotic and aristocratic party continued to be held against him for the rest of his life. His statesmanlike image was marred, too, by his weakness for high living and financial favors. Like Clay and Calhoun, Webster coveted the presidency, but his chances of winning it were even more remote than theirs. His constituency was a narrow one, and in any case someone who looked like God seemed rather out of place in the razzmatazz of an American presidential campaign.

Less formidable but more adroit was Martin Van Buren, who was more often associated with sorcery than with divinity. After the war the "Little Magician," as he was called, helped to build a powerful political machine in New York State known as the Albany Regency. By the 1820s, he was regarded as one of the most skilled political managers in the country. Van Buren argued unashamedly for the advantages of a party system and party organization at a time when most men still regarded parties as necessary evils at best. In New York, he showed what could be accomplished by a form of politics in which party discipline was put ahead of individual conscience. Slowly, the New York style of politics spread across the Union. Van Buren was the principal architect of the coalition which elected Jackson in 1828, and eight years later he succeeded the Hero in the White House. It was the Democratic party organization that he had helped to create, rather than his own popularity, that made Van Buren president—a fact which incensed his enemies. Martin Van Buren was the most abused public figure of his time. He was ferociously denounced as an "arch intriguer," a cunning and unprincipled political manipulator whose powers seemed almost to be rooted in black magic. Traditionalists blamed him for the new style of party politics, and his very skill caused him to be widely distrusted. Many felt that the election of a "mere politician" to the presidency was a mark of the degeneration of American political life. The charges of evasiveness and "non-commitalism" were not quite fair, for although Van Buren was unequalled in the arts of political management, he also remained true for most of his life to a Jeffersonian philosophy of government. He believed that the Union would best be served by a government with strictly limited powers.

## The Changing Political Landscape

The men who dominated American politics during the age of Jackson were obliged to come to terms with a new political environment. The game of politics was no longer what it had been in the days of Thomas Jefferson; the growing democratic sentiment and other pressures had introduced new rules.

One important change in the structure of American politics after 1815 was the disappearance of the old party system. For years, Federalists and Republicans had fought one another for control of government, but 1816 was the last year in which the ailing Federalist party was able to field a presidential candidate. This left the Republican party supreme in national politics. Many welcomed the demise of the old party system, feeling that partisan considerations distracted men from the national interest. President James Monroe looked forward to absorbing former Federalists into the government. Such an "amalgamation" policy, as it was called, would be eased by the fact that the Republican administrations had by now adopted several aspects of Federalist policy, notably a national bank, a moderate tariff, and increased expenditure on internal improvements and the armed forces. Noting the end of the old party warfare, observers dubbed the period the "era of good feelings." Actually, Monroe was not allowed to carry his amalgamationist ideas very far. Many of his supporters fiercely resisted coming to terms with the Federalists, whose devotion to free institutions they doubted. But the continued distrust of Federalism was not enough to keep the Republican party together; lacking a strong opposition, it began to dissolve into warring factions. It was widely assumed that this state of affairs would continue, and that future presidential elections would normally be contests between *several* leading Republicans. Such predictions, however, failed to note that the political landscape was also changing in other and more fundamental ways.

One feature of the new political environment was virtual universal suffrage—at least for white adult males. By European standards, American suffrage provisions had long been generous. But by the time Andrew Jackson became president, the few remaining restrictions on the exercise of the franchise by white men had been largely removed in most states. In this limited sense, democracy had arrived in the United States of the 1820s. The energies of the Jacksonian Democrats were thus not, for the most part, expended in giving the vote to the common man—he already had it. More energy was spent in winning that vote for themselves. In other ways, too, governmental institutions were made more democratic in order to retain public confidence. In a number of states in the 1820s, most notably New York, Virginia, and

*James Monroe gathered together a cabinet of high caliber. As president he adopted a largely self-effacing role in domestic affairs; his greatest achievements were in the realm of foreign affairs.*

Massachusetts, conventions were held to amend the state constitutions. In general, these tended to liberalize qualifications for voting and for office-holding, to limit the power of the executive, and to make representation fairer.

Perhaps even more significant were the changes that were being made in the method of electing the president, for in the Jacksonian era the presidential contest profoundly influenced politics at every level. Formally, presidents were elected by the electoral college, but the members of the college had themselves to be chosen. In some states, they had in the past been appointed by the state legislature, a procedure which denied to the people much of a voice in the election. In other states, electors were selected by the people, voting in districts. Each district chose one elector, which meant that the state's vote in the electoral college was often divided between the rival candidates. Yet other states used the general ticket system. This again allowed a popular vote, but on a statewide or winner-take-all basis, giving the victorious party all the state's electoral votes. States often changed from one system to another, and by the 1820s the lack of uniformity in the mode of electing the president was giving rise to considerable criticism. Election by state legislatures proved impossible to defend on democratic grounds, and was soon generally abandoned. At the same time, the general ticket system was increasingly adopted in preference to the district system, since a state exerted more influence in an election when its votes were delivered in a single bloc.

The triumph of the general ticket and of the popular election of presidents (or at least of their electors) had an important influence on the structure of Jacksonian politics. The procedure by which a president was elected largely dictated both the strategy that was to be adopted and the political machinery that was to be employed. None appreciated this more fully than the politicians themselves. In the decade after 1815, they engaged in a prolonged debate on the reform of the rules governing presidential elections, hoping thereby to promote the emergence of a healthier political system. Some, for example, feared that presidential campaigns would become conflicts between different sectional candidates and would eventually rip the nation apart. They wanted to structure the presidential contest in such a way as to alleviate sectional pressures. Martin Van Buren's suggestion was to adopt the district system throughout the Union, thus breaking up the large political blocs into small units. Others disliked the spreading general ticket system, since it meant that the campaign for a state's electoral votes would have to be conducted on a state-wide basis. This, they said, would encourage the emergence of party managers and manipulative techniques. They wanted to design the election rules in such a way as to avoid the need for organized parties, which, they felt, tended to put their own interests above those of the nation. But all these proposed reforms required constitutional amendments, and although Congress considered dozens of such amendments in the 1820s, it was unable to agree on any one of them and none were adopted. The general ticket system succeeded by default, bringing with it, some believed, evil consequences.

## Politics—American Style

One effect of the general ticket system and of the popular election of presidents was the emergence or strengthening of party organizations in the separate states, capable of conducting statewide campaigns. These party organizations normally communicated with the electorate via "official" newspapers, which the party usually found some way of subsidizing (often from public funds). These party organs were also weapons; the most savage political battles were daily fought out in the press. Throughout the Jacksonian period, the basic party units were the state or local organizations, which were forced into alliances with one another by the nature of the presidential contest. To win a majority in the electoral college, a candidate needed the electoral votes of several states, which meant cultivating the support of the several state organizations. Thus the national parties of the Jacksonian era can be regarded as loose coalitions of state parties. But just as candidates were interested in the backing of local machines, the machines were interested in the nomination of attractive candidates. Now that campaigns had to be taken to the people, they wanted candidates who would win votes.

The problem of how to select a presidential candidate was not an easy one. Somehow the scattered state parties had to be made to act in unison. Traditionally, the congressional caucus had chosen the candidate; that is, the party's senators and congressmen had met together to name their choice for president and vice president. There had always been doubts about the propriety of this procedure. But when the Federalist party ceased to function at the national level, criticism of the Republican caucus mounted. In the absence of an opposition party, the Republican congressmen were, in effect, choosing the next president. The undemocratic nature of the caucus system was a major issue in the campaign of 1824, and when most congressmen boycotted the caucus in that year they effectively destroyed it. John C. Calhoun and Martin Van Buren, among others, began to discuss the idea of a national convention to nominate candidates.

Although the first such conventions did not meet until 1831, they proved much more acceptable to Jacksonian America than the congressional caucus had been. The latter had seemed undemocratic and oligarchic, allowing a party's leaders in Congress to perpetuate power without reference to the people. The national convention, however, was democratic at least in form, consisting of delegates chosen by state and local conventions, or "fresh from the people," in Jackson's words. The convention was also a mechanism whereby the diverse elements within a party could act together.

While conventions were rarely models of democracy, they at least gave the party rank-and-file some voice in the selection of their leaders. Perhaps more importantly, in putting a premium on popularity they allowed men who had not served a long apprenticeship in politics—such as victorious generals—the opportunity to make a bid for high office. In this sense, the convention system helped to open up American politics, but only to a degree. The complex electoral and political machinery of this era also promoted the emergence of party professionals skilled in the techniques of manipulation. The cigar-chewing and cynical Thurlow Weed, powerful boss of the Whig party of New York in the middle decades of the century, was perhaps an unwitting model for the caricature of the party professional that was to be forever afterward associated with the American style of politics.

In other ways, too, American politics in the Jacksonian

era seemed to be diverging ever more sharply from the patterns of the Old World. While the Founding Fathers had undoubtedly created a new and distinctive system of government, the new political trends seemed to make it even more characteristically American. The power of the party managers rested in part on their control of the spoils system, which rewarded party loyalists with government offices and contracts. While not entirely new, under Andrew Jackson this practice became systematized at the national level. It was soon widely regarded as a necessary part of the governing process. It also exposed the Jacksonians to the charge that they were interested only in the spoils of office (not that their rivals were any less interested).

The wide suffrage and the high turnout at elections, particularly from the 1840s, were also distinctive features of American politics, and helped to introduce yet others. Party managers hunted for attractive candidates to present to this extended electorate, and those who seemed to spring directly from the people proved especially alluring. While Andrew Jackson was running for president, Davy Crockett, the quick-witted and colorful bear-hunter from Tennessee, was running for Congress. Both men capitalized on their homespun images. The need to arouse the enthusiasm of the large electorate generated a host of activities which particularly bewildered and entranced European observers. These included ebullient torchlight processions, festooned with defiant banners and political emblems; massive outdoor rallies, often simultaneously addressed by several orators in different parts of the ground; campaign songs and aggressive and soaring rhetoric; and rowdy scenes at polling stations, at which

*Electoral reform and a new generation of political leaders ushered in a growing public participation in American politics at midcentury. Bingham captures its spirit in this oil,* Verdict of the People, *painted in 1854–55.*

parties frequently posted brawny young men to clear the way for their own voters and to obstruct the enemy's. Many Americans themselves celebrated the emergence of what seemed to be uniquely American creations. In the decades following the War of 1812, and encouraged by that second rejection of British pretensions, a kind of xenophobic nationalism marked American political life. This led to a tendency to equate the truly American with the non-European. Andrew Jackson, it was pointed out when he first ran for the presidency, "was never in *Europe.*" This, it was implied, was a virtue: Europe had nothing to teach this rough-hewn son of the American frontier.

## New Parties are Born

The politicians of the 1820s thus found themselves in an uncertain and, in many ways, a novel political environment. But their primary obligation continued to be the protection and extension of American republicanism. For a while, it was hoped by many that this might be done without reverting to a party system. But this idea was reluctantly abandoned as new political parties began to develop. What is known as "the second American party system" functioned roughly from the late 1820s to the early 1850s. Its emergence was gradual. The presidential election of 1824 had been a contest between several members of the old Republican party. None had won an overall majority in the electoral college, although Andrew Jackson had won most popular and electoral votes. The election had, therefore, gone to the House of Representatives, where Henry Clay threw his weight behind John Quincy Adams, who was duly elected. Adams promptly appointed Clay secretary of state, and the incensed Jacksonians charged that there had been a "corrupt bargain" between the two.

The quarrel between the Adams administration and the Jacksonians realigned the various factions of the old Republican party into two opposing camps. The popular Jackson, who in Tennessee had not been particularly noted for his democratic sympathies, was now cast as the champion of the people. The groups outside the administration quickly lined up behind him. Martin Van Buren brought the powerful Albany Regency into the Hero's camp, and John C. Calhoun, although now vice president, also decided that his political future lay with the Jacksonians. The ideological differences between the administration and the Jacksonian opposition were by no means clear. Strong New England support for Adams and the adherence of Clay and Webster, however, suggested that the administration favored a positive role for the federal government in promoting economic development, while many of the Jacksonians were sympathetic to the states' rights position.

In 1828 there were thus only two candidates for the presidency, Andrew Jackson and John Quincy Adams.

This in itself was unusual, for the presidential campaigns of the 1820s and 1830s normally comprised several candidates. Not until the 1840s was the two-party system stabilized. The bipartisan fight in 1828 encouraged men throughout the nation to identify themselves either with the administration or with the Jacksonians. Party newspapers were established in Washington and in dozens of towns across the country, campaign biographies were published, and political broadsheets without number took the fight to the people. Party platforms were still a thing of the future in 1828. The Jacksonians promised only "retrenchment and reform," which meant reducing government expenditure and turning the "corrupt" Adams men out of office. They did not promise any systematic democratization of American politics.

The Jacksonian movement of the late 1820s combined tradition with novelty. Many of his supporters saw Jackson as sustaining the old Jeffersonian ideas of frugal government and states' rights. This image was rather blurred, for in some states Jackson was presented as an advocate of a more positive role for government. But in any event, he was cast as Jefferson's successor as the champion of liberty (which was said to have been threatened by the machinations of Adams and Clay) rather than as a radical crusader for democracy. His cause was said to be the old Republican cause, his mission to purify American politics rather than to transform it.

But while his partisans threw the mantle of tradition around Jackson's shoulders, his candidacy nonetheless marked a break with the past. Hitherto, every one of George Washington's successors in the White House had been either a former vice president or secretary of state,

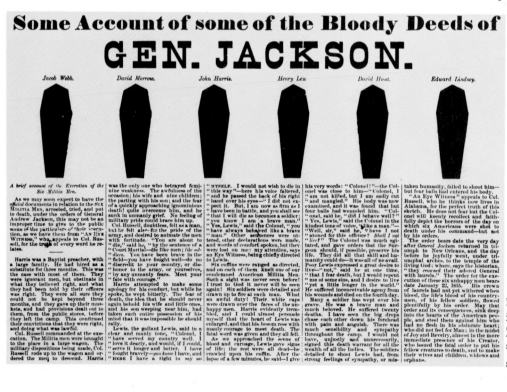

Not everyone worshipped Jackson as a hero. In his first election campaign this broadsheet was circulated by his political enemies. Known as the "Coffin Handbill," it refers to Jackson's supposed murder of militiamen during the War of 1812.

more often the latter. They had come from well-established Virginia or Massachusetts families, were highly educated and cultivated men, and had usually completed several years of distinguished public service before they were considered for the presidency. Jackson, by contrast, was from a state that had not even existed at the time of the Revolution. His education had been somewhat rudimentary, and his principal public services had been military rather than civil in nature. His critics held his lack of civil experience in particular to be a major weakness. To accept such a man as president meant abandoning the traditional ideas of the right qualifications for that office. The presidency was no longer to be reserved for those who had long proved their statesmanship.

In an age of popular elections, however, Jackson was a stronger candidate than his more sophisticated opponent. The son of the second president and a former Harvard professor, John Quincy Adams had served as minister to Russia and to Britain and as secretary of state before his election by the House in 1825. His partisans stressed his distinguished career in the public service, but the uncharismatic Adams aroused little enthusiasm outside his own New England. Jackson's friends made a

*John Quincy Adams was president from 1825 until 1829. But as chief executive he did not fulfill the promise of his earlier distinguished service as secretary of state.*

Fogg Art Museum (detail)

virtue of the rugged qualities of their candidate: ''Andrew Jackson who can fight; John Quincy Adams who can write'' rang one contemptuous boast.

The Hero of New Orleans won the election with 56 per cent of the popular vote, a proportion that was not to be surpassed in the nineteenth century. New Englanders overwhelmingly favored Adams, while Jackson met little opposition in many states of the South and West. In other words, while there were two candidates for the presidency, only in a few states did a two-party system actually function. Many Americans were still voting for their sectional favorites.

The party structure remained confused for some years. As late as 1831, Richard Rush, Adams's running mate in 1828, still believed that presidential elections would normally be contests between several rival candidates. The primitive state of the party organizations was reflected in their names, or their lack of them. In 1828 the Adams men were usually known as ''the friends of the administration,'' while their opponents were simply the ''Jackson party.'' By 1832, the Adams-Clay group were styling themselves ''National Republicans.'' The Jacksonians increasingly referred to themselves as ''Democrats,'' although the old term ''Republican'' was still frequently used by all groups.

By then, too, a new party had emerged—the Antimasons. Antimasonry had first sprung up in western New York in 1826 when William Morgan, a former Freemason who had written a book supposedly exposing the order's secrets, suddenly vanished. It was widely believed that Masons had silenced him by dropping him in Lake Ontario. Several northern states were soon shaken by a remarkable grassroots crusade to exterminate the monster of Freemasonry, whose secret ways were held to be a violation of American republicanism. Masons in government, it was believed, were using their sinister influence to advance the interests of their fellow members rather than of society as a whole. By 1832, the Antimasonic party was strong enough to run a candidate for president. Like the Jacksonians, the Antimasons believed that their mission was to purify the Republic, to remove the cancer that was eating into America's free institutions.

By the mid-1830s a degree of order was reached in the American party system. The Antimasonic party disappeared as a separate organization, partly because the number of Freemasons had dwindled rapidly. The party's leadership tended to be hostile toward the incumbent Jacksonians (Andrew Jackson himself was a Mason) and in several states they allied with the National Republicans, although they sometimes failed to carry their followers with them. By this time, too, many southerners who had helped to elect Jackson had now broken with him. They were followed by other southern advocates of states' rights and northern Democrats upset by various aspects of Jackson's policies. From these

*Freemasonry was a controversial movement. Left: Freemasons could claim many illustrious adherents, such as Washington, Jackson, and Lafayette. But the secretive organization was vigorously opposed in some quarters. Above: An Antimasonic tract publicizes the Freemason initiation ceremony.*

course of elections but who was never able to carry any state. In the end, the second American party system was unable to withstand the sectional pressure generated by the slavery issue. In the 1850s, the Whig party disintegrated and the Democratic party increasingly became the party of the South.

The election of 1840 marked the zenith of the second American party system. It was the first presidential election in which both major parties operated coherently at national, state, and local levels. It was the last in which the outcome was not significantly affected by the slavery issue. In 1840, nearly 80 per cent of the eligible voters actually went to the polls, a remarkable increase over the 55 per cent or so which had hitherto been the norm in the Jacksonian period. One reason for this dramatic upsurge of interest may have been the prevailing economic misery; there had been a financial panic in 1837 from which the economy had not yet recovered. The high turnout perhaps showed the popular faith in the ability of the political system to find a solution. Another reason was the close competition that now existed between the major parties in the great majority of states. Politicians now wooed the electorate more aggressively than ever before, generating an intense excitement which left few untouched.

## The Log Cabin Campaign

The Whigs had chosen for their candidate General William Henry Harrison, who was dubbed "Old Tippecanoe" after his best-remembered military victory. Henry Clay had wanted the nomination, but in the course of his long career he had inevitably offended some parts of the electorate. Harrison was deemed more "available." In order to satisfy their southern wing, the Whigs nominated John Tyler of Virginia, a states' rights advocate, as their vice-presidential candidate. They then flung themslaves into one of the most colorful campaigns of all time, using every device to stampede the people into voting for "Tippecanoe and Tyler too." Responding to a Democratic gibe that the elderly Harrison would be content with a pension, a log cabin, and a barrel of hard cider, the Whigs trumpeted that their candidate did indeed embody the simple virtues associated with the log cabin and hard cider. They exploited this image for all it was worth. Massive outdoor rallies were held throughout the country, some lasting for days and attracting tens of thousands of participants, who had often traveled hundreds of miles to attend. Women and children also frequently attended these extraordinary celebrations. With their fervid oratory and their enthusiastic rendering of campaign songs, the rallies sometimes took on the flavor of religious revivals. The enthusiasm to turn the "spoilsmen" out to make way for honest Old Tippecanoe was infectious.

dissident groups a new party eventually emerged—the Whig party. Composed of former National Republicans, Antimasons, states' rights advocates, and disgruntled Democrats, it maintained a precarious unity through the common hostility of its elements to Andrew Jackson and all he stood for.

With each succeeding presidential election, the two-party system spread to yet more states. By 1840, the two major parties had vigorous organizations functioning in most areas. There was also a small third party, the Liberty party, a product of the antislavery movement. This pattern survived until the mid-1850s. In these years, presidential elections were contests between the nominees of the Democratic and Whig parties, who between them always won every electoral vote. They were accompanied by the candidate of a smaller anti-slavery party, whose presence certainly influenced the

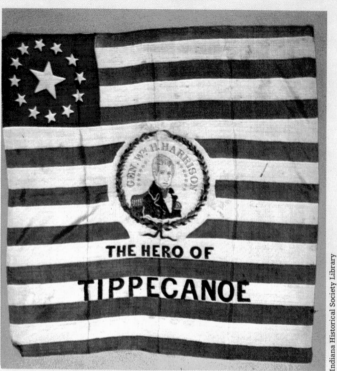

The presidential contest of 1840 was dubbed the Log Cabin Campaign. According to the Democrats, the Whig candidate, William Henry Harrison, would be more at home in a log cabin than the White House. The Whigs turned the jibe to their advantage, arguing that their candidate embodied the simple virtues of frontier life. Harrison (far left) had come to prominence in 1811 with his victory at Tippecanoe—an achievement which became central to his presidential campaign nearly thirty years later. Even special music was used to praise the aging hero. The Democrats could not put a foot right. They alleged that Harrison had a penchant for strong drink, but this backfired as the Whigs turned this, too, to their advantage.

The evangelical zeal of the Log Cabin Campaign was sharpened by the hard times, from which people wanted deliverance. The Democratic administration was blamed for this continued economic depression, and Van Buren was again the party's flagbearer in 1840. Unlike the Whig national convention, the Democratic convention had adopted a platform—one which generally favored a strict construction of the Constitution and a limited role for government. Such policies, however, had not rescued the country from financial chaos. So in 1840 a majority of the voters put their faith in the amiable old hero of Tippecanoe, who was elected decisively. However, in the course of giving his inaugural address—the longest in American history—Harrison caught a cold. One month later, the Whig savior was dead. He was succeeded by his running mate Tyler. But Tyler's states' rights sympathies rapidly alienated the bulk of his party, which found itself once more gnashing its teeth in opposition.

## Sectionalism and the "Bank War"

The relatively small role played by slavery in the 1840 campaign illustrates one feature of the politics of the Jacksonian era—the widespread desire to play down divisive sectional issues. The party leaders knew that to win a presidential election a candidate must normally secure votes from both North and South. They were anxious to avoid sectional conflict. In some measure, the national parties of the Jacksonian era were constructed precisely in order to keep sectionalism at bay. Martin Van Buren attributed the strong sectional friction of the 1820s to the disintegration of the old national parties. In 1827, he urged the reconstruction of a political coalition embracing "the planters of the South and the plain Republicans of the North" as a means of promoting friendlier relations between the sections. Slavery did not seriously come between the major parties of this era; the parties conspired to exclude it as a political issue.

When sectionalism did reach a crisis point in 1832 it was in spite of the efforts of the party leaders. The "tariff of abominations," passed four years earlier, had placed high duties on certain farm and manufacturing products of the North and West, to the fury of southern planters. South Carolinian planters in particular were experiencing hard times, largely because of the falling price of cotton and the poor quality of their overworked land. They blamed their plight on the tariff. They were also highly sensitive to any threat to slavery, and were anxious to resist anything which might tend to increase the power of the federal government at the expense of the individual states. South Carolina's politicians began to ask whether they could justify Congress's "plundering" or whether they would be better off outside the Union. Vice President

John C. Calhoun, sensing the growing states' rights sentiment in his home state, abandoned his youthful nationalism and became the foremost spokesman for southern rights. He resigned from the vice presidency in order to lead the states' rights movement as a senator for South Carolina. The Constitution, he claimed, was a compact between sovereign states. These states retained their sovereignty, and if their agent, the federal government, exceeded its powers, then the state could nullify the government's power within the state's boundaries. And as a last resort, if the federal government attempted to force its jurisdiction on the state against its will, the state could withdraw from the Union as easily as it had joined.

In 1832, Congress passed a new tariff bill which did little to assuage the bitterness of South Carolinians. On November 24, a state convention declared that the tariff act was "null, void, and no law, nor binding upon this State, its officers or citizens." They threatened to take the state out of the Union if the federal government tried to use force to collect the tariff.

President Jackson responded swiftly. He strengthened forts, ordered government revenue ships to collect the tariff, and prepared to send an army into South Carolina if necessary. At the same time, South Carolina began raising a volunteer force to repel any federal "invasion." The stage seemed set for the civil war which politicians had striven so hard to avoid.

In the end, the confrontation was narrowly avoided. On January 21, 1833—less than two weeks before South Carolina's nullification ordinance was to go into effect—plans to lower the tariff were announced in Congress. South Carolina responded by suspending the nullification ordinance. The tariff bill was signed by Jackson on March 2, together with a bill authorizing him to use force, if necessary, to collect this new tariff. The promised reductions in the duties placated the South Carolinians, who finally repealed the original nullification ordinance. At the same time, however, they nullified the new Force Act. This was merely a face-saving gesture, for the Force Act was no longer needed. The sectional issue of the 1830s was thus settled by a compromise, but the underlying dilemma—states' rights versus the preservation of the Union—was left unresolved.

The other major issue of the Jacksonian era was the "Bank War." The Bank of the United States had been functioning for some years as the country's central bank, but its mammoth capital ($35 million) and the continued fluctuation in the value of paper money caused it to be viewed with grave suspicion by many. Jackson himself disliked banks and the paper currency they churned out. In 1832, Henry Clay persuaded the bank to seek a new charter, expecting that Jackson would not dare to veto such a move in an election year. But Jackson accepted the challenge, vetoed the bill, and in the next year took the war a stage further by withdrawing government

*The "Bank War" created havoc among businessmen and financiers. This 1833 cartoon, the "Downfall of Mother Bank," symbolizes the disruption which followed Jackson's removal of government funds from the Bank of the United States.*

deposits from the bank. These measures enraged Clay and his associates, for they regarded a strong national bank as indispensable to the country's economic welfare. Jackson also attempted to suppress small bank notes and to encourage the circulation of hard money, or specie. The Van Buren administration continued the attempt to divorce banking from government. When financial panic overtook the nation in 1837, the Whigs blamed it on the financial policies of the Jacksonians, while the latter attributed it to the speculative ventures of the monied interests.

In the course of the 1830s, the major parties thus became associated with contrasting economic and political philosophies. The Democrats argued that the principal threat to American republicanism came from a financial aristocracy, which was attempting to win control of the country through the Bank of the United States and the Whig party. Bank charters and other economic legislation, they charged, were designed to confer privileges on the rich at the expense of the many. The Whigs, for their part, denounced the Jacksonian policies as reckless. Economic prosperity, they believed, brought benefits to everyone, and required a strong banking and credit system and the protection of growing industries. The true threats to American republicanism, the Whigs argued, were the corruption associated with the spoils system and the dictatorial tendencies of Jackson and his Democratic

successors. Jackson's methods during the Bank War had been somewhat high-handed, and the Whigs charged him with "executive usurpation"—treating the other branches of government with contempt as he transformed himself into "King Andrew." The enlargement of the powers of the presidency, in their view, was at the expense of the liberties of the people.

The Whig party often fared well in urban and economically advanced areas, while the Democrats were strong in rural and isolated areas. This pattern was not a clear one; the Democrats also usually carried certain large cities. But the Whigs tended to be the spokesmen for the entrepreneurial spirit, welcoming the growth of industry and commerce. They claimed that all classes would benefit by economic expansion and diversification. The Democrats, on the other hand, acted as the spokesmen for those who were uneasy about the erosion of the old agrarian order under the impact of the burgeoning commercial and industrial enterprise. They feared that the "moneyed aristocracy," symbolized particularly by banks, was using its power to exploit the ordinary

35

*Entitled "King Andrew the First," this cartoon appeared in 1833 when Jackson refused to extend the charter of the Bank of the United States. His critics claimed he was acting like a tyrant king.*

people. Commercial expansion and urban growth were destroying the agrarian republic of the past. They were also promoting class antagonisms which threatened the social fabric. The Democrats kept alive the old Jeffersonian concept of government and society. They stoically resisted the economic changes that were transforming the world around them.

## Preserving the Union

Economic issues thus figured prominently in the party battles of the Jacksonian era, though the issues themselves were often symbols for larger visions of American society. The quarrels over banks and internal improvements served to disguise one hard fact of American political life —the pressure of sectionalism. While the major parties tried to avoid open conflict over slavery, sectionalism nonetheless was an important part of the political culture of the day. Its impact was indirectly felt on presidential elections, for example, in the kinds of standard-bearers the parties chose. The most successful candidates were prominent generals with relatively nonpartisan images. As victorious soldiers, they had established their patriotism and won admirers throughout the Union. Their relative inexperience in politics (one of them, Zachary Taylor, had not even voted before) meant that they had not made themselves unacceptable to any section by identifying themselves with particular issues. Another category of candidate who had not made implacable sectional enemies was the "dark horse"—the candidate who unexpectedly emerged from relative obscurity to win his party's nomination. With the single exception of Martin Van Buren, every successful presidential candidate during the period of the second party system was either a military hero or a dark horse.

In contrast, the men whom European visitors regarded as the greatest statesmen of the day, most notably Clay, Calhoun, and Webster, found that the presidential prize unfailingly eluded them. The penalty of political prominence was "unavailability." Such men had inevitably offended some important section or class. The major political parties were precarious coalitions of sectional interests, and they best survived in a democratic environment by avoiding divisive issues and agreeing upon inoffensive candidates.

The major parties saw their own integrity as necessary to the survival of the Union. The men who had scrambled onto the political stage at about the time of the War of 1812 had assumed a formidable trust. It was their duty to protect and perpetuate the American experiment in republican government. Cynical and opportunistic as some of them were, many retained a genuine concern for their country's welfare. They worked to adapt American institutions to the advance of democracy, hoping thereby to strengthen the inheritance of liberty. They sounded the alarm at every threat they spied to their society of free men. The Antimasons perceived a threat in Freemasonry, the Democrats in the "Money Power," and the Whigs in presidential usurpation and the spoils system. While the politicians of this era were operating in a more democratic environment than their predecessors, their central purpose of carrying forward American republicanism remained the same.

To this generation of political leaders, or at least to most of them, republicanism was synonymous with union. The destruction of the Union would entail not only the separation of the states but also, in all probability, anarchy and despotism. While they disagreed over methods and warred over contrasting economic and social philosophies, they also tried to fashion a system of politics which would keep the nation together.

# Chapter 3

# THE LAND OF OPPORTUNITY

*"The notion of labor is therefore presented to the mind, on every side, as the necessary, natural, and honest condition of human existence." Tocqueville was by no means the only visitor to note the American passion for work. A new land meant a new life and the hope of betterment—for native Americans as well as the new arrivals from Europe. With the industrial drive came the need for improved lines of transport and communication, so work began on a network of roads, canals, and railroads. Distances were reduced as the nation began to be drawn together. Though life out West was still, for many, relatively simple, society as a whole was each day becoming more and more sophisticated.*

# The Rewards of Industry

I should want to work moderately but resolutely at least fourteen hours of each secular day, until I had made myself comfortable, with a fence around at least eighty acres, . . . a tolerable habitation for my family, at least forty acres in crop, and a young orchard growing. For one commencing with next to nothing, I estimate this as the work of five years; after which he might take things more easily, awaiting the fruit from his orchard and the coming up of his boys to help him. But for the first four or five years, the poor pioneer should work every hour that he does not absolutely need for rest.

This extract, from journalist Horace Greeley's *An Overland Journey* (1859), was written two and a half centuries after the first settlement of America. Nevertheless, it tells the story of much of American experience to that date. In the attempts of the first colonists to make a new life for themselves in their new environment, or the struggles of the nineteenth-century frontiersman to tame the western wilderness, we find the same pattern. Hard labor, frequent failure, and occasional disaster combined to bring the settler a meager reward.

Sloth was literally the deadliest sin. The alternatives, often enough, were work or die; leisure time was non-existent, self-indulgence a form of suicide. Work was both the greatest leveler of men and the greatest selector of the fittest. Time was the most valuable commodity. Every daylight hour had to be put to fullest use; there were always more jobs than hours—so much to do, so little time to do it in. The family was the work unit whose purpose was self-sufficiency, with a division of labor between male and female. The man's domain was outdoors, where there were always trees to be felled and logs to be sawn, buildings to be erected and improved, and tools to be made. Land, too, had to be broken, seed to be sown, crops to be harvested, and animals to be fed, delivered, or slaughtered. There were also roads to be cleared and laid, a well to be dug, a stream to be dammed,

*Sloth, children were told, would not be endured in America. "What a sight! The sluggard stretched out while mother and sister work busy as bees. Let him lose his breakfast and he will learn better ways."*

a millstone to be hauled. Self-sufficiency required the man to be a jack-of-all-trades, as English journalist William Cobbett described the farmers of Long Island in 1818: "His *skill*, the versatility of his talent is a great thing. Every man can use an *axe*, a *saw*, and a *hammer*. Scarcely one who cannot do any job at rough carpentering, and mend a plough and wagon. Very few indeed, who cannot kill and dress pigs and sheep, and many of them oxen and calves. Every farmer is a *neat* butcher; a butcher for *market*. . . . All are ploughmen. In short, a good laborer here, can do *any thing* that is to be done upon a farm."

But the women, in their indoor realm, had to be similarly versatile. A Swiss immigrant in 1823 described them as follows: "They take care of everything pertaining to the domestic economy, for example making candles, boiling soap, preparing starch, canning berries, fruit and cucumbers, baking, spinning, sewing, and milking the cows."

The sense of urgency never vanished. Once families had been housed and could feed themselves, there were larger tasks to be undertaken. Cities and factories had to be built, canals to be dug, railroad tracks to be laid, steamboats and locomotives to be made and fed with fuel, raw materials to be produced and processed. Time remained precious. The same Swiss migrant was told: "Smoking a pipe is too much trouble. We have other things to do than spend time stuffing and cleaning a pipe."

Similarly a German settler, Francis Grund, wrote in 1839: "The habit of eating against time exists only in America."

Or, as John D. Rockefeller himself later lamented: "Work by day and worry by night, week in and week out, month after month. . . . I sometimes wonder how we came through."

There were, in 1815, about 7 million white Americans and 1.5 million black Americans. Half the white population was under fifteen years of age, and had thus been born in the nineteenth century; almost 5 million were under twenty-five years of age and therefore born after George Washington became the first president. These were the very young people of a very young nation, not colonists or immigrants but a generation of *Americans* rapidly growing to maturity. Perhaps 1 million, aged over forty and thus born before the Declaration of Independence, would be able to remember the first inauguration.

The astonishing youthfulness of the population was its leading characteristic; one in three was a child under ten years old. This meant that the potential work force was correspondingly small. To do the work and produce the goods for the entire population, there were about 1 million male whites and under half a million male blacks in the prime years of 16 to 45, approximately one producer to three or four dependents. In some areas, particularly those settled about a decade earlier where the children were still young and the wives preoccupied with their upbringing, every adult male might have four, five, or six dependents—and dependent in a quite literal sense. Family size, as the Greeley quotation implies, was often crucial in helping a man make a success of his venture. A man's farm was his factory and his family his work force. Children were welcomed because, although they were extra mouths to feed, they would eventually provide extra hands to share the work. With "the coming up of his boys," as they became strong enough to help with the heavy work, the burdens of the farmer at last began to be shared. But the nagging sense that there was always work to be done remained. Large families rarely removed the sense that labor, like time, was always in short supply and therefore valuable. Skills were greatly prized: "He who can make a pot himself and mend his own pants and shoes counts far more than a foppish little gentleman, even one with money, who tries to keep his hands soft in his pockets. . . . All honest work is worthy of recognition; only his own ineptitude holds a person back." Richard Cobden encountered an Irishman in 1835 who "talks of his son who is a clever scholar and of the respect he will meet with in America for his talents though he be not rich, whilst in Britain his abilities without wealth would be neglected."

## Meeting America's Labor Shortage

All writers agree that America suffered all through this period from a serious shortage of labor. This scarcity was met in two main ways. First, when need arose, there were neighbors willing to help. The rugged individualism of the pioneer has often (and rightly) been stressed by later writers. But the extent of community cooperation was as frequently observed by contemporary visitors: "The kind of hospitality that here was given to complete strangers was extended in Europe only to one's dearest friends. . . . It meant companionability, amiable familiarity, neighborly concern over another's well-being, generosity with advice, and practical aid in building a new neighbor's house or husking his corn." There were experiments in communitarian living where such cooperation was the rule. But it was not only in such organized communities that tasks beyond the strength of single families, from road building to harvesting, were performed with mutual aid. Neighborliness meant a willingness to share, advise, help, and if necessary, rescue.

The second solution was to stretch human ingenuity to its utmost in attempts to develop implements and machinery to make human effort more effective. The simplest of tools devised by Americans were able to excite the admiration of the European as works of art: "The axe here . . . is a combination axe, wedge and sledgehammer;

To get the work done, very often whole communities joined forces. The term "bee" came into use, as the workers were as busy as those in a hive. Right: The quilting bee was a useful opportunity to exchange news and gossip while working at the same time. It often took weeks to make one quilt. Far right: Meanwhile, the men work together to erect a new neighbor's house. Below: Not a dance or a fight, this is a scutching bee. Members of a Pennsylvania community are seen preparing flax for weaving into linen. Scutching consisted of beating the flax to rid it of wooden fiber.

Museum of the City of New York

National Gallery of Art, Washington, Gift of Edgar William and Bernice Chrysler Garbisch

what an accomplished woodchopper can do with this instrument! There are some among them who can chop and split five and a half loads of wood a day, including stacking them.''

There is thus a direct connection between this labor shortage and the development and application of technology in America. A machine was to be regarded as man's friend and assistant, not as his enemy. It not only increased his output but also made his life easier by taking the toil out of human labor. Implements were devised to enable one man working alone to accomplish what would otherwise have required a gang. Hence the development of machinery for farm and industry, powered by animals, water, and steam to supplement man's own muscular energy.

## Town and Country

The vast majority of the population in 1815 still lived on farms, either in the small single-family units of New England or the Northwest or on the larger plantations of the South. Most of these farms, moreover, were primarily concerned with survival and self-sufficiency. They were not producing cash crops to sell in the market. Nevertheless any opportunity would be seized to exchange things produced and not required for things required and not produced. These included items provided by the wildlife of the forest and the lumber (in one form or another) cleared to make way for crops, as well as the surplus produce harvested in a good year. For if you could not sell, you could not buy. And so long as you could not buy, your equipment and the raw materials for your house and equipment, as well as your food and clothing, were restricted to what you could produce yourself. ''Living off the land'' was limited by what the land provided.

The likeliest prospect of profitable exchange was offered by a nearby town or by the development of some mode of transport which gave access to a town. Towns, although few in number, were growing rapidly. New York and Philadelphia in 1815 were cities of over 100,000; Baltimore and Boston were around 50,000. These cities were growing very rapidly indeed. Between 1790 and 1820, New York and Philadelphia maintained growth rates of over 50 per cent per decade. This speed exceeded that of all British cities at the height of the Industrial Revolution. The decade of the 1840s saw total urban population grow from under 2 million to over 3.5 million; this increase of 92 per cent was the greatest urban growth in any single decade in all American history.

Another feature of American towns in the first half of the nineteenth century is that there were a few large rather than many small ones. By 1860, there were in the United States eight towns with populations of over

41

# Americans at Play

Americans enjoyed many forms of recreation. Left: The cold winter months in the Northeast and Midwest provided opportunities for skating. Winslow Homer painted this Central Park skating scene in the winter of 1859–60. Below left: John B. Rich Institute for Physical Education was one of the first American public gymnasiums. This lithograph dates from 1850. Below: An exclusively male audience watches a bare-knuckle boxing tournament.

The St Louis Art Museum

Collection of Edgar William and Bernice Chrysler Garbisch

# The World of Fashion

Godey's Lady's Book *set the fashion for mid-nineteenth century American women. Opposite top: The frontispiece of an 1843 issue portrays what women that year would wear for evening entertainment in the home. Bottom: Costumes for the opera and warm winter outfits. Below: Men, too, were conscious of their dress. These gentlemen appear in the latest London fashions for the summer of 1845.*

# The Evening's Entertainment

*Dancing was a favorite form of entertainment for both the sophisticated city-dweller and the rough-and-ready frontiersman. Right: Elegant couples dance the polka, newly imported from eastern Europe. Below: A convivial rustic dance. Opposite: New Yorkers pack the city's Park Theater for an evening of comedy in November 1822.*

*The invention of the steamship revolutionized*
*travel. Pictured here is the* Clermont, *built*
*by Robert Fulton, steaming its way up*
*the Hudson from New York City past West Point.*

be so reduced, and goods traffic mainly consisted of small valuable objects; cheap, bulky, heavy products simply could not bear the cost of transport.

Roads came first, initially no more than Indian trails or paths cleared through the forest to make haulage easier. Then methods of improving the surface and drainage were developed. By 1815, a fairly wide network of turnpike and other roads had evolved. The construction of the National Road (also called the Cumberland Road, but further north than Daniel Boone's Cumberland Gap) began in 1811. It ran across the Appalachians from Cumberland, Maryland, to Wheeling on the Ohio River and was eventually extended to Vandalia, Illinois. The National Road was financed by the federal government and made with a foundation of fifteen inches of crushed stone with a macadamized surface, and was thirty feet wide. Private turnpike companies, levying tolls on all passing travelers (exactly like modern toll highways for automobiles, but much less successful in the collection) proliferated between 1790 and 1830. Some 400 such companies were founded in New York, Pennsylvania, and southern New England, and they built and operated over 4,000 miles of road. Few of these turnpikes were profitable, and the technical problem of creating an all-weather, all-traffic surface remained unsolved. One partial solution to these difficulties was the cheaply constructed plank road, created simply by laying heavy planks over a smoothed surface. These greatly facilitated traffic, especially for short-haul farm carts.

The first significant improvement in transport came with the application of steam power to river transport. As early as 1787, John Fitch had demonstrated his paddle boat on the Delaware River to members of the Constitutional Convention. But it was in 1807 that the most important development took place, with the first journey of Robert Fulton's steamboat *Clermont* from New York to Albany. It made the journey of 150 miles in thirty-two hours. Very soon, a regular passenger service was established between New York and Albany. For many years, however, the extension of steamboat traffic on eastern rivers was held back by the restrictive patent granted by the New York legislature to Fulton and Robert R. Livingston, his business collaborator. Fulton and Livingston had a monopoly for twenty years on the waters of New York State. But the Supreme Court, in the case *Gibbons* v. *Ogden*, declared that the patent was an unconstitutional invasion of the right of the federal government to control interstate commerce. With the defeat of the Fulton patent, steamboats developed rapidly on the inland waters. Already, in 1811, the steamship *New Orleans* had left Pittsburgh, where she was constructed, and sailed to the mouth of the Mississippi in just over ten weeks. The river boats used timber for fuel, and the woodpile at every landing came to afford a hiding place for escaping Negro slaves. The Mississippi steamboats became the major form of transport in the West. Above all, they permitted return journeys upstream. Old Muddy was a treacherous river with snags galore, and the boat engines themselves had a notorious habit of exploding. The journey was hazardous and exciting but, as if to compensate, the boats became sumptuous and the passengers affected an imposing gentility.

The most important transport breakthrough in nineteenth century America, however, was the canal. The famous Erie Canal led the way, and its impact was immediate and dramatic. The port of New York was at once linked directly with Lake Erie, above Niagara Falls, and thus with the entire midwestern hinterland. Branch canals gave access to Lake Ontario at Oswego and Rochester, and the Champlain Canal continued north from Albany. While the canal certainly facilitated the movement of people to the midwest, the biggest advance was in the carriage of goods in both directions. Farmers could now send to the eastern markets their grain, potatoes, meat, and other produce; Buffalo rapidly grew as the main flour-milling center in America. Heavy goods could now be transported west—machinery, furniture, hardware of all kinds, as well as cloth, clothing, and a wide variety of imports. The farmer was no longer dependent on what he could produce for himself. Division of labor and specialization in production at last became a reality.

The evident success of the Erie Canal led many other states and cities to attempt to follow New York's lead. A frenzy for "internal improvements" swept through America for the next decade. The year of the Erie's completion saw the state of Ohio embark on two canal projects to link the Ohio River with Lake Erie. Further west still, both Indiana and Illinois began to lay plans for extensive building.

In 1826, Philadelphia, alarmed by the boost given by the Erie to New York's commerce, persuaded the Pennsylvania legislature to provide funds for an ambitious transport scheme to the West. This project, however, had to rise to over 2,000 feet to cross the Allegheny ridge. From Philadelphia, a horse-drawn railroad traveled some 80 miles to Columbia on the Susquehanna; from there, a canal followed the Juniata for 173 miles to Hollidaysburg, where the 36-mile Allegheny Portage Railroad took over.

The canal boats were mounted on railroad cars which were pulled by horses along the level stretches of country between five inclined planes. The cars were dragged up the inclines by means of stationary steam engines pulling cables on drums, until they finally "rested on the top of the mountain at Blair's Gap like Noah's Ark on Ararat, and descended next morning into the valley of the Mississippi and sailed for St Louis!" In this way, the boats were raised and lowered over 1,000 feet. The ten engines which were installed at the five summits all bore the insignia "Made in Pittsburgh." On the western side, a canal conveyed the boats 105 miles to Pittsburgh.

In the South, Virginia and Maryland combined to build the Chesapeake and Ohio Canal, but this venture was only completed as far as Cumberland and never reached the Ohio.

The effects of the canals are much debated. There can be no doubt about the unparalleled success of the Erie. Other eastern canals were financial failures, but they gave access to the coal fields of Pennsylvania and facilitated distribution of that bulky commodity to eastern industries and cities. Ohio's two major canals contributed to the agricultural development of a vast terrain, both through settlement and the transport of produce to New York via Lake Erie and the Erie Canal. Indiana's Wabash and Erie Canal was sanctioned in 1836 in the state's mammoth Improvement Bill. When completed in 1843, it permitted the 240-mile journey from Lafayette to Toledo to be completed in two days and eight hours. But the Wabash and Erie Canal came too late; railroads were already spreading rapidly. Like so many other canals, it was a financial failure, though its contribution to the opening up of the state was inestimable.

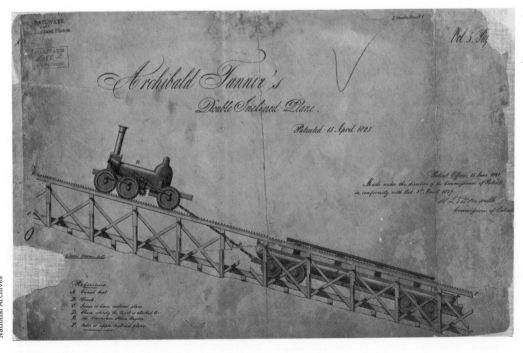

*Archibald Tanner designed this double-incline railway, powered by a locomotive, for transporting barges over hilly terrain.*

# The Erie Canal

In the early part of the nineteenth century America caught a new disease . . . "Canal Fever." This contagion, the sudden boom in canal construction, was the result of the first canal in America—the Erie Canal, built between 1817 and 1825. It began from a shallow ditch that ran between Buffalo, at the mouth of Lake Erie, and the town of Albany on the Hudson River. This was to become the path of the longest and most spectacular man-made waterway of its time.

De Witt Clinton, the governor of New York who launched the project, vowed he would "make the desert bloom like the rose." That was in 1817. Nine years later the completed canal stretched 363 miles, with 18 aqueducts and 83 locks—the most advanced, at Lockport, cut in the side of an escarpment of granite.

In fact, most of the construction was done by amateurs, local farmers working in their spare time. Even the two chief architects, John Geddes and Benjamin Wright, were ignorant of canal construction when the project started. The best advice they could get came from Irish laborers. These had been brought specially from England for their experience during the canal boom there.

The problems were acute. Water, it became depressingly clear, tended either to evaporate or drain away. On the first completed section the water level dropped alarmingly—nearly two feet per week. Then someone discovered that a nearby local slime, "the blue mud of the meadows," cut the loss by half if it were smeared thickly on the canal wall.

Work went on, but now beavers interfered. Their damming was relentless. Hours were wasted in clearing the blockages and debris—longer if the canal sides burst.

When, in 1825, the canal was at last

finished, the populace from Buffalo to New York City celebrated. Their festivities were lavish, extravagant, bizarre. The longest canal deserved the longest cannon salute in history. For one hour and twenty minutes, on October 26, 1825, a chain of cannon was fired, each within earshot of the next, down the length of the canal and all the way to New York Harbor. Then, for good measure, the whole operation was repeated backwards.

But the most dazzling and unusual episode was the ceremony named the "Wedding of the Waters." Two wooden kegs were filled, one with water from Lake Erie, the other with waters of the great rivers of the world, including the Mississippi, the Nile, the Ganges, and the Thames. The kegs, small enough for a man to carry, were taken to Buffalo to be put aboard the *Seneca Chief*.

Then, on November 4, a flotilla of small craft set out from Buffalo with the *Seneca Chief* at their head. They sailed the canal to Albany, down the Hudson River, and from there to Sandy Hook at the mouth of New York Harbor. Once in the bay they were joined by a huge and colorful array, boats of all sizes flying innumerable flags and streamers, while from the shore · the sound of church bells and cannon fire rolled out across the waters. There, as the sun rose, Clinton held up each keg before him and emptied its contents into the Atlantic Ocean. This act was to be a symbol, both of the union of the Great Lakes and the Atlantic, and of free navigation and commerce throughout the world.

The canal was a monument of some beauty, but it was not all romance. Shortly after its completion, English writer Frances Trollope (mother of novelist Anthony) completed a pleasure cruise down the canal as a highlight of her holiday. She wrote bluntly: "I can hardly imagine any motive of convenience powerful enough to imprison myself again in a canalboat."

*Left: The opening of the Erie Canal, America's first of its kind, warranted a celebration. And one took place in New York Harbor on November 4, 1825, shown here alive with ships in full flag dress. Top: Lockport was the scene of a unique combination of locks built into steps of granite. Above: Rochester was one city that grew up and prospered in the wake of the Erie which flowed through the city center.*

## Birth of the Railroad

Boston did not build canals. The Berkshires, the Green Mountains, the White Mountains all presented apparently insurmountable barriers to canal building, though there were paper projects in large numbers. It was, in fact, in Boston that the first American railroad was laid in the early 1820s, though not yet using steam locomotion. In 1826, T. H. Perkins secured a state charter for his "Granite Railroad." This was designed to transport granite from a quarry three miles away for the Bunker Hill monument. The foundation stone of the monument had been laid by the aged Marquis de Lafayette, accompanied by President John Quincy Adams, in 1824, almost half a century after the battle.

In June, Perkins visited Darlington in England to inspect the Darlington and Stockton railway, opened two months earlier. A master mason, Gridley Bryant, with no previous knowledge of railroads built Boston's railroad with the labor of 150 men in about six months. The cars were long platforms suspended from four wheels, each over six feet in diameter. The cars weighed a ton and a half and a "train" of three cars carrying sixteen tons of granite was

pulled on wood and iron rails by a single horse. Unlike the British prototype, the Granite Railroad had to anchor the rails below the frost line because of the heavy burden. To do this, Bryant sank dry stone walls three feet deep. Granite ties, weighing a ton or more, were laid across these walls every eight feet. The "rails" were pieces of pine lumber a foot high surmounted by small oak beams and a bar of rolled iron. The horse walked between the rails, the car wheels having iron flanges to keep them on the iron straps. Because of the drop of eighty-six feet in the line, a strong braking system was necessary. The Granite Railroad eventually carried some 12,000 tons of granite before the monument was finally dedicated in 1843 (with a two-hour speech by Daniel Webster).

In June 1827, a delegation of the General Court of Massachusetts visited the Granite Railroad. Shortly after this, they voted to begin a railroad survey for their state. Baltimore, too—like Boston, left behind in the canal race —quickly decided to proceed with railroads, and the Baltimore and Ohio Railroad was chartered in 1827.

The first trial run of a steam locomotive was in 1829 when the "Stourbridge Lion," from England, was tested on the gravity railway of the Delaware and Hudson Canal Company. In May 1830, the B & O opened the first thirteen miles of track in America using steam locomotives. By the end of that year, seventy-three miles of railroad were in operation. That the South was still enterprising is revealed by the major initiative taken by Charleston merchants in building a railroad to its cotton-raising hinterland. When completed in 1833, the Charleston and Hamburg Railroad (Hamburg being on the South Carolina bank of the Savannah River, opposite Augusta,

*The first railroads were designed to link nearby towns and improve existing means of transport for goods and passengers. This painting shows the engine* Planet *in 1834, some four years after steam engines were introduced.*

ENGINES OF THIS PLAN WEIGHING FROM 37000 TO 64000 LBS.

M.W. BALDWIN & CO, LOCOMOTIVE BUILDERS,
PHILADELPHIA.

Georgia) was 136 miles in length—by far the longest in the world.

By 1840, over 3,000 miles of railroad had been built and the railroad had already proved its ability to cross the mountain barrier. These early railroads were built quickly and cheaply. The idea was to get something moving, making the improvements later. Most joined existing towns and were designed to improve existing traffic. But others often passed through remote, isolated areas, injecting life wherever they penetrated. The track was crude, the bridges fragile, the safety precautions primitive. A journey by train could be an exciting adventure. Charles Dickens described it vividly:

The train calls at stations in the woods, where the wild impossibility of anybody having the smallest reason to get out, is only to be equalled by the apparently desperate hopelessness of there being anybody to get in. It rushes across the turnpike road, where there is no gate, no policeman, no signal: nothing but a rough wooden arch, on which is painted "WHEN THE BELL RINGS, LOOK OUT FOR THE LOCOMOTIVE." On it whirls headlong, dives through the woods again, emerges in the light, clatters over frail arches, rumbles upon the heavy ground, shoots beneath a wooden bridge, . . . suddenly awakens all the slumbering echoes in the main street of a large town, and dashes on haphazard, pellmell, neck-or-nothing, down the middle of the road. There—with mechanics working at their trades, and people leaning from their doors and windows, and boys flying kites and playing marbles,

*Locomotive building soon became a lucrative business. Matthias Baldwin built Pennsylvania's first railroad engine in 1832, and went on to found the world's largest locomotive manufacturing company.*

and men smoking, and women talking, and children crawling, and pigs burrowing, and unaccustomed horses plunging and rearing, close to the very rails —there—on, on, on—tears the mad dragon of an engine with its train of cars; scattering in all directions a shower of burning sparks from its wood fire; screeching, hissing, yelling, panting; until at last the thirsty monster stops beneath a covered way to drink, the people cluster round, and you have time to breathe again.

A further 5,500 miles of railroad were added in the 1840s to bring the total to nearly 9,000, but with four-fifths still in the seaboard states. The 1850s was a decade of particular significance in the history of American railroads. No less than 20,000 miles were added in those brief years, mostly completed before the panic of 1857—at a time when the population was under 30 million. By 1860, there were five times more miles of railroad per person in the United States than there were in Britain. Traffic to the Mississippi and beyond was established; Chicago was linked with New York; the Illinois Central was built. In 1859, Richard Cobden observed in his diary: "After passing 20 or 30 miles [from Chicago] we came upon the Great Prairie over which the road [the Illinois Central] was carried four years since, when there was scarcely an inhabitant upon it. Now it is dotted with small farm houses. . . ."

In the same year, 1859, Horace Greeley was able to travel by rail as far west as St Joseph, just north of Kansas City. With the end of the line came the end of civilization. Having left New York on May 9, he was already in Chicago on May 12 and St Joseph by May 14, about 1500 miles in six days. But thereafter his progress by wagon was slow. He did not reach Pipe Creek, Kansas, 150 miles away, until two weeks later. He recorded the fast disappearance of the amenities of life:

| | | |
|---|---|---|
| May 23rd—Leavenworth. | Room bell and baths make their final appearance. | |
| 24th—Topeka. | Beefsteak and washbowls (other than tin) last visible. Barber ditto. | |
| 26th—Manhattan. | Potatoes and eggs last recognized among the blessings that "brighten as they take their flight." Chairs ditto. | |
| 27th—Junction City. | Last visitation of a boot-black, with dissolving views of a board bedroom. Beds bid us good-bye. | |
| 28th—Pipe Creek. | Benches for seats at meals have disappeared, giving place to bags and boxes. We (the two passengers of a scribbling turn) write our letters in the express wagon that has borne us by day, and must supply us lodgings for the night. Thunder and lightning from both south and west give strong promise of a shower before morning. Dubious looks at several holes in the canvas covering of the wagon. Our trust, under Providence, is in buoyant hearts and India-rubber blanket. | |

## New Networks of Communication

Internal transport improvements constituted the major, but not the only, element in improved communications. The year 1818 saw the establishment of regular, scheduled sailings by the Black Ball Line from New York to Liverpool. At precisely 10 AM on January 5, dead on time despite a snowstorm, and with a minimal cargo of apples and seven passengers, the *James Monroe* left its mooring on the Hudson River. Just over three weeks later, she arrived in Liverpool, having crossed in mid-Atlantic with her counterpart, the *Courier*, which had left Liverpool on January 4 laden with textiles and other manufactured goods.

In the 1820s, the Black Ball Line offered two scheduled sailings a month in each direction. Before long, several other "liners" were in operation. The size of the vessels used at first was little greater than those in use a century earlier. But by the 1850s, a new, beautiful, and much bigger kind of sailing ship, the famous Yankee Clipper, of over 1,000 tons, dominated the North Atlantic. Clippers were also used in the China trade, especially after 1849. In that year, England repealed her navigation laws and allowed foreign ships to carry tea from the Orient to English ports. Clippers were also prominent in the carriage of passengers and freight to California (16,000 miles via Cape Horn) in the gold rush of 1849, and to Australia in the 1850s.

The building of seagoing vessels was concentrated above all in New York, where there were thirty-one ship-building yards in 1855, but also in Boston. In a large number of small towns on the coast of Maine, the whole seaboard population worked at crafts associated with the sea: ships' carpenters, sailmakers, riggers, ropemakers. Of 100 vessels registered in New York in 1850, three-quarters had been built in New England and about half of these in Maine.

In 1853, Commodore M. C. Perry arrived in Tokyo Bay, Japan. In the following year he signed the Treaty of Kanagawa, the treaty of friendship and trade between Japan and the United States. Another chapter had opened in the story of American commerce.

American mercantile dominance, dependent on the superiority of the clippers, was, however, already confronted by the threat which would eventually destroy it. In April 1838, two British-built vessels, the *Sirius* and the *Great Western*, arrived in New York Harbor within a few hours of each other. Both had crossed the Atlantic with the aid of steam-driven paddle wheels; the latter vessel had crossed in $14\frac{1}{2}$ days. The first regular Cunard steamer, the *Britannia*, left Liverpool on the Fourth of July 1840. Still more ominous was the arrival in New York in 1845 of the *Great Britain*, an iron-hulled steamer of over 3,000 tons equipped with a screw propeller. On January 1, 1848, two Cunard liners sailed simultaneously from Liverpool and New York, and the British bid for the North Atlantic traffic was unmistakable. In 1851 the *Baltic*, a vessel of another British company, the Collins Line, reduced the Atlantic crossing for the first time to under ten days.

Another innovation, the telegraph, links the two themes of railroads and transatlantic communication. It was in 1835 that Samuel Morse first transmitted the sound of dots and dashes by means of an electric battery. Nine

# Perry's Gunboat Diplomacy

Since the mid-seventeenth century, Japan's only contact with the West had been through limited trade with the Dutch. In the sixteenth century she had been on good terms with other Western nations, notably the Spanish and Portuguese. But fear of Western inroads on Japanese society had led her to adopt a policy of national seclusion. The Dutch were allowed to continue trading because they did not engage in missionary work.

In the early years of the nineteenth century, with the Napoleonic wars raging in Europe, Dutch ports were closed and the traders were being forced to charter their ships elsewhere. Some of them were chartered in the United States, and the American crews, returning home with tales of the riches of this largely unknown land, aroused the interest of merchants and traders. At the same time, American whalers from the Pacific fleets pressed the government for protection from the Japanese, who had repeatedly maltreated shipwrecked crews, and in 1851 Congress finally voted to seek diplomatic relations with Japan.

For safety's sake, the American message to the emperor (a letter written by President Fillmore) was to be transported by a naval squadron.

Chosen to lead the expedition was Commodore Matthew Calbraith Perry, a man with forty years of naval experience, and an expert at handling steamships. After eighteen months of preparation, Perry left Norfolk, Virginia, on November 24, 1852, in command of the steam frigate *USS Mississippi.* Other vessels were ordered to join him on the way, and on July 8, 1853, he led a fleet of four ships into Tokyo Bay. As they neared the shore, the Japanese made signs for them to disperse. Perry merely pointed to his guns, and the Japanese made no further resistance to his entry.

When Perry explained that he had come to deliver a letter to the emperor, the Japanese were horrified. The emperor was politically no more than a figurehead, but the Japanese believed that he was a descendant of the sun god. Therefore, it was inconceivable that a bullying foreigner could be allowed to meet him, whatever the foreigner's intentions. Not even the country's feudal oligarchs would consent to meet the commodore. Perry soon began referring to himself as an admiral in hopes of more

success, but the Japanese responded by dressing up minor government officials with fanciful titles like "the First Councillor of the Empire." On July 14, Perry announced that he would return the following year for an answer to the American request.

Perry and his crew spent the fall and winter exploring the coast of Japan. Whenever a Japanese appeared hostile, the commodore either pointed once again to his guns or marched a contingent of marines onto Japanese soil. It quelled hostility every time.

When Perry returned to Tokyo Bay in February 1854, he was greeted much more warmly. A reception was arranged at Yokohama on March 8, with feasting and an exchange of gifts. The Japanese presented Perry with quiet tokens of friendship—silks, porcelain, and lacquerware. The commodore was disappointed; the gifts did not match the monetary value of his own, which were embarrassingly comprehensive. The most ambitious was a quarter-scale railroad, on which the American sailors whirled the Japanese around a miniature track at fifteen miles per hour. This example of American technology delighted the hosts, as did the gift of some Colt pistols. Perry also presented them with several illustrations of America's recent military victories, as a not-too-subtle reminder of the danger of opposing United States foreign policy and trading claims.

The commodore was equally disappointed by the Japanese trade concessions. He had set his sights on at least five harbors, but he was only granted entry to one—Nagasaki, where the Dutch were already trading. After a few more unsubtle suggestions from Perry, the Japanese relented and formal agreement was signed providing for American outposts in the ports of Hakodate and Shimoda. They also promised protection for all American ships and sailors in distress on the high seas.

Perry failed to realize that these seemingly minor privileges represented an important change in Japanese thinking as well as in their country's foreign policy. Japan had no desire for contact with the West; it was Perry's constant show of force alone which prised the doors open. The expedition was a major triumph for American mercantile policy, and paved the way for great increases in trade with the Far East. But the Japanese people did not forget their first contact with the Americans, and Perry's bullying tactics left a legacy of misunderstanding and mistrust which was to influence relations between the two countries for many decades.

All pictures: Collection of the Chrysler Museum at Norfolk, Va

*The Japanese commemorated Perry's visit in the paintings of the American delegation seen here. Left, from top: Perry himself, secretary and Dutch interpreter H. Portman, and Japanese interpreter Wells Williams, who disapproved of the commodore's blustering manner. Above: Captain Joel Abbot. Right: Perry announces to a Japanese official that he has a letter for the emperor. Behind him, American ships lie at anchor in Tokyo Bay. Below: Sailors demonstrate their miniature railroad at Yokohama in March 1854.*

Peabody Museum of Salem/Markham W. Sexton

Peabody Museum of Salem/Markham W. Sexton

Courtesy United States Naval Academy Museum

*Perfected in the 1850s, clippers were developed
from smaller vessels (known as "Baltimore
clippers") built a half-century before. Above:*
*The* Golden West. *Below: Clippers in Boston Harbor.*
*Right: Builders took pride in their ships' figureheads.*

*Above: Samuel F. B. Morse, appointed art professor at the University of the City of New York in the early 1830s, had to wait for the completion of new buildings before he could begin teaching. Meanwhile he worked on his new invention, the telegraph. With the introduction and spread of the telegraph came the expansion of newspaper publishing. Below: Catching up with the news in a New York boarding house.*

years passed before the telegraph was sufficiently developed for the first experimental telegraph line to be strung between New York and Washington, but during the mid-1840s the commercial application of the telegraph began in earnest. Used at first mainly for railroad signaling, and greatly assisting the efficiency of railroad operations, the telegraph was often built alongside the tracks. Nevertheless, it took far less effort to build and quickly overtook the railroad in mileage. By 1860, an extensive network of over 50,000 miles of telegraph had been set up.

The spread of the telegraph is also closely linked with the development of newspapers and magazines. This was linked in turn with the extension of general education and literacy in the 1820s and 1830s. A landmark was the founding in 1841 of the *New York Tribune* by Horace Greeley, the circulation of which soon rose to nearly 250,000. In the Census of 1860, as many as 20,000 workers were recorded in the trades of "Printing and Publishing." Journals were also beginning to appear and circulate widely; 1857, for example, saw the first appearance of *The Atlantic Monthly* and *Harper's Weekly*. The role of the written word as a causal factor in the American Civil War can hardly be exaggerated. Nevertheless, mass circulation newspapers in the modern sense were still in the future.

## The Industrial Work Force

By the eve of the Civil War, although manufacturing had spread far beyond its original narrow confines, about three-fifths of all manufacturing production was still concentrated in five states. Industry gave employment to over 1.2 million persons, or about 12 per cent of the total labor force of 10.5 million. New York, Pennsylvania, and Massachusetts each employed 250,000; Ohio and Connecticut together accounted for a further 140,000. But in the *intensity* of industrialization—the number employed in manufacturing in relation to the total labor force—Massachusetts and Connecticut have a long lead over all other states. By this criterion, Rhode Island also has to be included among the top industrial states.

The leading industries at midcentury were still mainly concerned with the early processing stages of raw materials. Industries concerned with the provision of clothing were the largest employers of labor. The footwear, clothing, and cotton textile industries each gave labor to over 100,000 persons. A further 50,000 were employed in the woolen and worsted industry and in leather manufacturing. In addition, the iron industry gave work to 65,000, and the timber industry to 75,000.

Manufacturing provided employment for just over 1 million men and 250,000 women. The three industries employing the largest work force also had the greatest number of female employees: in the making of clothing, two-thirds of the labor force was female and large numbers were also employed in the footwear and cotton textiles industries. Another industry providing female employment was the woolen industry where half the labor force was female; "hats and caps" production and paper manufacturing together accounted for 8,000 women.

The conditions of employment of these women workers in American industry, especially in textile factories, caught the attention and admiration of many British visitors. Harriet Martineau, for example, waxed lyrical in her description of these "Ladies of the Loom" and the window boxes of flowers in the factory windows. Under the "Waltham system," named after the Massachusetts town where it was introduced, the textile companies provided well-supervised boardinghouses, insisted on

*Right: Bookbinding and other light industries employed many women. Below: A title page from* the Lowell Offering, *a publication produced by women factory workers in Lowell, Massachusetts.*

LOWELL OFFERING

November, 1845.

*" Is Saul also among the prophets?"*

A REPOSITORY
OF ORIGINAL ARTICLES, WRITTEN BY
"FACTORY GIRL."

LOWELL: MISSES CURTIS & FARLEY.
BOSTON: JORDAN & WILEY, 121
Washington street.
1845.

education and religious observance, employed only girls of good character, and endeavored to create "model" conditions of work in the factories themselves. Charles Dickens found in 1842 that 978 factory girls had joint savings of $100,000 in the Lowell Savings Bank. Three aspects of their lives particularly appealed to him: many of the boardinghouses had a well-used "joint-stock piano"; most of the girls subscribed to circulating libraries; and they published their own periodical, the *Lowell Offering*, "a repository of original articles written exclusively by females employed in the mills."

These excellent conditions of work reflected the general labor shortage discussed earlier. Positive inducements were needed to entice girls to take on factory work. Most of the employees were farmers' daughters who stayed in the factories for a few years only, then returned to their former rural life. Factory work was not their livelihood, merely an episode in their lives. They did not constitute a permanent wage-earning labor force. There was still "the Great West open for our girls away there, with all this clamor for teachers, missionaries and wives," as wrote the editor of another factory periodical, the *New England Offering*.

By the late 1840s, this predominantly female work force in the factories began to give way to a more permanent type of wage earner. This above all consisted of the recently arrived Irish immigrants, but also of other "low-class New Englanders" as they were described in the same *New England Offering*. By 1860, the character of the textile work force had markedly changed. A different environment had come into being, and this was to become more predominant in the post-Civil War years.

Most industries were fairly well dispersed among the leading industrial states. Half the footwear industry was in Massachusetts; about one-quarter of clothing was in New York. The southern New England states provided the main center for cotton textile production, based on water power, but Pennsylvania and New York also had well-developed industries. The new but rapidly developing iron industry, found mainly in Pennsylvania and New York, was beginning to grow in Ohio.

In concentrating on the leading states, we should not overlook several lower down the list. The presence of Ohio in the top five is an example of industrial development outside the original thirteen states. Further west, Illinois and Indiana both had industrial work forces of over 20,000.

Even Virginia had the beginnings of a cotton textile industry as early as the 1850s—enough to make an observer in the *Economist* note that, if its development continued, "grass might soon be growing in the streets of both old Manchester [England] and new Manchester [New Hampshire]." Virginia had 37,000 industrial employees in 1860.

Mining activities also provided significant industrial employment in certain states. In Pennsylvania, anthracite coal mining already had a labor force of 25,000, larger than any other industrial activity. California appears in the list of mining states in 1850 through the considerable labor force devoting itself to the search for gold.

Coal production, however, was not yet at a level to permit its universal use in industry, transport, or for domestic purposes. Until the 1880s, coal remained less

important than other energy sources, particularly wood for transport and water for industry. Similarly, despite its recent, rapid expansion, the iron industry was still unable to meet America's requirements. The largest single import from Britain in the 1850s was iron rails for the massive railroad-building program of that decade. Most agricultural implements were still made of wood, although the production of agricultural machinery was an area in which iron was beginning to transform America.

## *"Yankee Ingenuity" Makes Its Mark*

Yet in significant directions, manufacturing technology was moving ahead rapidly. The characteristically American exhibits at the 1851 Great Exhibition in London were all regarded as examples of Yankee gadgetry. These included, above all, such essentially labor-saving machinery as the McCormick reaper (first patented in 1834 but produced by factory methods in Chicago after 1847) and

*McCormick's reaper greatly increased efficiency in harvesting. The testing of the first reaping machine near Steele's Tavern, Virginia, in 1831 is the subject of the watercolor below.*

Courtesy Chicago Historical Society

the Howe sewing machine (first patented in 1846). But the history of American applied technology dates from the first decade of the 1800s when the principle of interchangeable parts was applied to firearms production; Simeon North and Eli Whitney both claim credit for this.

Several others made their contribution to what came to be known as "the American system" of manufacturing. This was the name given to the production by specialized machinery, operated by unskilled workers, of standardized parts made with sufficient precision to be assembled into the required final product. Its main application and development continued in the firearms industry. John H. Hall made important improvements in accuracy through his metal-cutting and woodworking machines at Harpers Ferry Armory; Samuel Colt applied those methods with still greater precision at his Hartford armory in 1855. The advance in metallurgy and precision instruments allowed similar methods to be applied to clock making, and then to products of greater accuracy and delicacy such as sewing machines and watches. The American Watch Company was established at Waltham, Massachusetts in 1848 and developed the production of watches by machinery. During the 1850s, the US Patent Office granted over 2,500 patents per year. Isaac Singer improved upon Howe's invention, and by the middle 1850s the sewing machine had become the first important piece of household machinery to come into widespread use.

Not all the results of technology were such delicate products. In 1839, Charles Goodyear had invented the vulcanization of rubber, and by 1850 a rubber industry was manufacturing heavy rubber footwear, such as overshoes and knee-length boots. Beginnings were being made in food preservation and, although canning factories were not opened before the Civil War, the principles of sterilization were generally known. Gail Borden patented the process of condensing milk for canning in 1856.

It would be wrong to assume that these inventions resulted from systematic research. Essentially, the final result emerged from a nearly universal search to improve methods of production. "Every workman," wrote an English merchant, "seems to be continually devising some new thing to assist him in his work." Just as the problems of building the Erie Canal were overcome almost yard by yard, as they occurred, so minor improvements here and there, as well as the major inventions, all contributed. An American writer could claim in 1835:

> It thus appears that in every department of the cotton manufacture, there is an economy of labor greatly exceeding that of England. . . . The perfection to which machinery has been brought, enables the proprietor to avail himself much more extensively of female labor than is the case in Europe. The labor of females is . . . much more productive, and they consequently receive higher wages. The males . . . are not compelled to compete with machinery,

are enabled to apply their powers in other ways that are more productive, and as a consequence, when they marry the necessity for the employment of their wives and young children in factories is unknown. . . . A still further consequence is, that the state of morals at Lowell, Dover, Providence, and other places where extensive factories exist is such as is almost unknown in any other part of the world, and constitutes a phenomenon . . . equal to that of Niagara in the natural world. . . . The necessity for the passage of "Factory Bills" does not exist in this country.

*New inventions changed the shape of the American economy. Above: A demonstration of Isaac Singer's improved sewing machine. Below: Rubber boots, part of an industry that sprang up after Goodyear's discovery of the vulcanization process.*

LONG ELASTIC TOP BOOT. This style is superior to any other long top boot for gentlemen, as it has a light, elastic close-fitting leg, not requiring the aid of straps to hold it up. Price, per pair, $5.50.

Men's Long Top Boots, $5.50.      Men's Knee Boots, $5.00.

| | |
|---|---|
| Boys' Boots, Sizes 1 to 6, | $3 00 |
| Youths' Boots, Sizes 13 and under, | 2 00 |
| Ladies' Boots, Felt or Wool Lined, | 2 50 |
| Misses' Long Boots, Felt or Wool Lined, | 1 75 |
| Misses' Long Boots, Net Lined, | 1 63 |

Yet the industrial scene at midcentury was complicated. Alongside these technologically advanced industries, a great deal remained highly primitive. Many items of production were, as yet, beyond the capabilities of American industry. Much was still done in the home or workshop by crude, unskilled performers. Distribution problems still remained acute, so that the advantages of the new developments had a restricted scope. The final products were, often enough, crude but utilitarian, lacking all style and embellishment. Charles Dickens gives an amusing account of his encounter with a boot maker whom he requested to make a copy of the boot he was wearing:

> He turned it over and over; surveyed it with a contempt no language can express; and enquired if I wished him to fix me a boot like that! "And this" he said at last "is a London boot, is it? This is a London boot, eh? . . ." He mused over it again, after the manner of Hamlet with Yorick's skull. . . . "You an't partikler about this scoop in the heel, I suppose then" he says; "we don't foller that here. . . ." He rose, put up his pencil, notes and paper . . . put on his hat; drew on his gloves very slowly; and finally walked

*J. W. Ehninger's* The Yankee Peddler *shows how the selling of new wares still relied on old methods of distribution. The peddler displays a new type of coffee grinder to New England women.*

out. When he had been gone about a minute, the door re-opened, and his hat and his head reappeared. He looked around the room, and at the boot again, which was still lying on the floor; appeared thoughtful for a minute; and then said "Well, good afternoon." "Good afternoon sir" said I: and that was the end of the interview.

And the end of new boots for Mr Dickens.

The foregoing survey of industry in 1860 has emphasized its heavy concentration in a small number of states. This is only one example of the many regional diversities which existed in the 1850s. The South, with its plantation economy and slave labor system, forms a major exception to many of the generalizations put forward in this chapter. The Old Northwest, the Old Southwest, the Far West, and the intermediate settlements such as the Mormons in Utah or the unsettled mountain men, all had their own very different characteristics. Although many writers have discussed at length the condition of *the* American economy on the eve of the Civil War, this is as much a chimera as *the* American. Obviously, the transport developments discussed earlier were already doing much to bring about a greater integration of Americans into something that might be called an American economy. But that integration was very far from complete in 1860, for the American people were still "on the move," and immigration was bringing changes, not only in the nation's economy but in its way of life as well.

# People on the Move

Journeying along the National Road to Illinois Territory in 1817, Morris Birkbeck, an immigrant from England, found himself part of a throng of westward-moving pioneers from the eastern states. "Old America," he observed, "seems to be breaking up and moving westward. We are seldom out of sight, as we travel on this grand track to the Ohio, of family groups behind and before us." To Birkbeck, it seemed that America was one "vast hive" and that restlessness was a national characteristic. Americans, he wrote, "are a migrating people, and even when in prosperous circumstances can contemplate a change of situations which, under our old establishments and fixed habits, none but the most enterprising would venture upon when urged by adversity."

The scale of the westward movement was not the only evidence of the migratory disposition of Americans. There was also the exodus then in progress from the farms to the expanding cities. This drift to the cities, especially marked in New England, was due chiefly to the rise of the factory system. Until 1830, when immigration from Europe began to rise sharply, the New England textile factories had to depend for their labor upon the native farm population. The same was true of the manufacturing and commercial enterprises in New York, Philadelphia, and other seaboard cities. And even when European immigration assumed mass proportions, the city continued to be a magnet for thousands of American country dwellers.

Even so, it was the West that lured most of those who left their homes in eastern rural areas in the years between 1815 and 1850. Not that there was anything new about the westward surge of population. Americans had been on the move, mainly toward the West, ever since the founding of Jamestown two centuries earlier. But in 1815, the agricultural frontier had advanced less than half the distance across the continent. Much of the territory between the Alleghenies and the Mississippi still remained to be occupied. The settled area of the United States lay almost wholly within a westward-pointing triangle whose base was on the Atlantic coastline and whose apex was at the confluence of the Ohio and the Mississippi rivers. On either side of this triangle lay two huge provinces, stretching respectively to the Great

*With white settlement went the need for land. While most Indians were cajoled into parting with their land and moving elsewhere, the Seminoles in Florida refused. Below: Seminoles attack a fort during the 1835–42 war.*

Library of Congress

Lakes and the Gulf of Mexico. These were the areas into which land-hungry settlers were to pour in the next quarter-century. By 1850, the pioneer vanguard would be everywhere well beyond the Mississippi. In addition, a number of outposts would have been established on the Pacific coast.

The movement into the interior was not a continuous march, but a fitful series of waves. The sudden rushes of boom years were invariably followed by a drying-up of the stream in periods of depression. Thus the wave of settlers which swept into the West immediately after the War of 1812 receded during a depression which began in 1819. Regaining momentum in the late 1820s, the movement suffered a further check during the depression years of 1837–40 before rising to a climax at midcentury. In the process, the nation's center of gravity had moved several hundred miles to the west. Whereas in 1810 only one American in seven had lived west of the Appalachians, by 1850 the figure was almost one in two. In the same period, the primeval forests and rolling prairies of the Ohio and Mississippi valleys had been transformed into a land of farms and plantations.

The advance of white settlement could not have taken place without the subjugation of the Indian tribes and their removal from their ancestral homes. The War of 1812 cost the Indians much and weakened their ability to resist. Tecumseh's death at the Battle of the Thames removed the only leader capable of uniting the northern tribes. In addition, Britain's withdrawal from the area south of the Great Lakes meant that in future the tribesmen would be unable to turn to a foreign power for help against the United States. In the Southwest, the red man had been weakened by internal divisions and cowed by Andrew Jackson's victory over the Creeks at the Battle of Horseshoe Bend in 1814. Thus the way was open for the extension of federal control over the tribes, and for increasingly peremptory demands that they give up their lands east of the Mississippi and move farther west.

By a mixture of bribery and threats, most of the tribes were prevailed upon to sign treaties ceding their lands. In return, they received annuities and presents or the promise of new lands west of the Mississippi. But some tribes resisted removal and were forcibly ejected. The removal policy led to two Indian Wars—the Black Hawk War of 1832 and the Seminole War of 1835–42. The former conflict, in which Abraham Lincoln served as a private in the Illinois militia, was no more than a series of skirmishes against the confederated Sacs and Foxes. But the Seminole War involved full-scale operations in the Florida swamps and cost the United States 1,500 men and $50 million.

The worst example of ruthlessness was provided by the state of Georgia in the 1830s when it expelled the Cherokees. Despite a decision in their favor by Chief Justice John Marshall in the case of *Worcester* v. *Georgia*, the Cherokees were denied the protection of the federal government. Nor did the fact that they had embraced white civilization save them. A systematic campaign of harassment and discrimination led by state officials culminated in 1838 in their being driven from their homes at the point of the bayonet. About a quarter of the Cherokees died as they straggled across the Mississippi to join the other evicted eastern tribes.

The cruelty and injustice of the removal policy was strongly condemned by a minority of northeastern congressmen and by New England intellectuals like Ralph Waldo Emerson. It also was bitingly criticized by foreign visitors such as Alexis de Tocqueville. He remarked ironically that the removal of the Indians had been accomplished "with singular felicity; tranquilly, legally, philanthropically. . . . It is impossible to destroy man with more respect for the laws of humanity." But this was not a viewpoint shared by many Americans. Land-hungry frontiersmen and other advocates of removal argued that the Indian was an obstacle to progress and a dangerous menace to the safety of the white man. It was left to President Jackson, however, to provide the most hypocritical justification for Indian policy. Removal was in the Indian's own interests, he declared, because they were unhappy living among white men. Moreover, they were threatened with extinction.

## Roads to the West

What facilitated the growth of new western settlements, and in many instances determined their location, was the remarkable improvement in transportation in the early nineteenth century. In the seaboard South, settlers had three roads to choose from. The Great Valley Road ran parallel to the Appalachians, then led through the gaps in the mountains to the Tennessee Valley and to Memphis. The other two roads, the Fall Line Road and the Upper Road, both followed southwesterly courses from Maryland before converging at Columbus, Georgia. There, they formed the Federal Road which ran on to Mobile and to Natchez. Farther north, emigrants bound for the Ohio Valley had an equally wide choice. Those from New England and New York could follow the Mohawk and Genesee Turnpike from upstate New York to Lake Erie, or cross the Hudson at Albany and take the Catskill Road to the headwaters of the Allegheny. From eastern Pennsylvania, the most convenient route lay along the Lancaster Turnpike and the old military road to Pittsburgh. But no other land route could compare with the celebrated National Road. Thousands of pioneer families moved annually along its 834-mile length, traveling by horseback, stagecoach, or Conestoga wagon and accompanied by droves of cattle and hogs.

But even when traveling on the new turnpikes, settlers could still get bogged down in a mudhole in bad weather and possibly lose a wagon. Besides, the cost of hauling household possessions and farm equipment overland remained relatively high. Hence emigrants still preferred, wherever possible, to travel by water. They were therefore quick to take advantage of the facilities offered by the Erie Canal. Almost overnight, the canal became the most popular route to the West. The horsedrawn barge superseded the covered wagon as the characteristic mode of emigrant transportation.

Steamboats too, at least across the Great Lakes, were quick, reasonably comfortable, and above all cheap. Competition was so keen that passenger fares and freight levels fell to a fraction of their former levels; deck passage between Buffalo and Detroit, for instance, cost only about $3 in the 1830s. It is hardly surprising that the emigrant stream was deflected from the Ohio Valley to the Great Lakes. By midcentury, emigrants from New England and the Middle Atlantic states, having colonized Ohio, Indiana, and Illinois, were pressing forward into Michigan and Wisconsin and even venturing beyond the Mississippi into Minnesota.

## A New Agricultural Pattern

The main causes of migration from the seaboard states were the development of the factory system and the growth of cities in the first quarter of the nineteenth century. These provided New England farmers with what they had hitherto lacked—a local market for specialized crops. The result was that many abandoned subsistence farming for more profitable but less labor-intensive forms of agriculture. Yankee farmers located near expanding cities turned to vegetable growing and to dairying. Those in the Connecticut Valley switched to tobacco growing and those in hilly country to sheep raising. The "sheep craze" which swept over Massachusetts, Connecticut, and Vermont in the late 1820s was a major cause of rural depopulation. As had happened earlier in the Scottish Highlands, the introduction of sheep led to the consolidation of small farms and to the wholesale conversion of arable land to pastoral, with a consequent shrinkage in the demand for farm labor.

Tending still more to dislodge New Englanders from their homes were the ruinous effects of western competition. Every new western farm, every inch of highway and canal linking the Atlantic Seaboard with the interior, made the lot of the New England farmer harder. The rocky, sterile soil of New England could not hope to compete with the rich, virgin lands of the West. Once the road and canal network across the Appalachians was complete, New England farmers entered an era of adversity. As cheap farm products from the Ohio Valley flooded into eastern markets in the 1840s, the price of both grain and wool plummeted. In the face of such difficulties, thousands of New England farmers had no alternative but to pull up stakes and either seek jobs in nearby mill towns or head west to begin farming afresh. The whole of New England was affected by this upheaval. But its effects were most marked in the marginal farming regions—the Berkshires, the Green Mountains of

*The Frederick Road, running inland from Baltimore to the Alleghenies, was one of the routes taken by a swarm of settlers who struck out for a new life in the West. After a long day, dusty and fatigued, travelers looked forward to the hospitality of the inn before continuing the journey next day. This painting is by Thomas C. Ruckle.*

*Left: An early photograph*
*of a farmer feeding his sheep.*
*The spread of sheep raising*
*in New England caused a drift*
*to farmlands farther west.*
*And as the fertile Ohio Valley*
*became productive, eastern*
*farmers lost trade and*
*faced stiff competition.*
*Below: A Cincinnati market*
*scene painted by Henry Mosler.*

Vermont, and the hilly country of New Hampshire and Maine.

In the Middle Atlantic states, too, agriculture felt the impact of western competition. The consequences were not as severe as in New England, because the soil was better and because the section was strategically located for feeding the growing numbers of city dwellers. Many farmers in New York, New Jersey, and Pennsylvania turned profitably to dairying, market gardening, and fruit growing. But even in these states there was a good deal of agricultural distress.

The most striking examples of agricultural decline were in the seaboard South. Here the effects of western competition were heightened by soil exhaustion. The earliest examples of worn-out soils were in Virginia, Maryland, and North Carolina. There tobacco had been grown, year in, year out, for more than a century, with no attempt to diversify crops or conserve the soil by scientific methods. The same wasteful methods of cultivation prevailed in cotton-raising regions. By the 1820s, these methods had left a legacy of declining crops and exhausted fields throughout the Piedmont areas of Georgia and the Carolinas. Pleas of agricultural reformers for an end to a system that butchered the soil fell largely upon deaf ears. There was, after all, little incentive to adopt scientific farming when the rich alluvial soil of Alabama and Mississippi lay within easy reach.

The farmers and planters who pushed the southern frontier westward made the transfer to the Gulf Plains with ease. The soil was better suited to cotton than the uplands of Georgia and South Carolina, and could be more easily cultivated. Nor did the first settlers in the Old Northwest face unfamiliar problems. The thickly wooded lands of the Ohio Valley could be cleared and farmed in much the same way as in New England or Kentucky. But the grassy prairies of Illinois were a different matter. Here there were no forests to supply wood for homes and farms, few streams to provide water. Worse still, the tough prairie sod could not be broken by the wooden plows most pioneers were used to. New techniques had to be employed to make cultivation possible. Wood had to be hauled in, wells dug, and a heavy steel plow developed. Pioneering on the prairies was thus an expensive business, but once the initial sod breaking had been accomplished and a "sod crop" raised, wheat could be grown with little effort. And once the Erie Canal brought eastern markets within reach, the prairie farmer found that profits would justify the heavy capital expenditure.

## Settlements on the Frontier

The distinguishing feature of the westward movement was its spontaneity. It was essentially an undirected migration of individuals who moved wherever their inclinations led them. Compared with the migration of colonial days, there were relatively few movements of groups or communities. But the pattern of settlement was nevertheless influenced by the federal laws regulating the sale of public land. From the Revolution to the Civil War, there was continual controversy over public land policy, especially over land prices, terms of sale, and squatters' rights. The Land Act of 1796 favored large land companies at the expense of settlers. It provided that public lands be sold at auction in large tracts (640 acres) at a minimum price of $2 per acre. After Jefferson's election in 1800, however, this Federalist measure was repeatedly amended. The minimum unit of sale was reduced, first to 320 acres and then to 160 acres. Purchasers were allowed several years to pay. Installment buying, however, encouraged a riot of speculation, and in 1820 Congress abolished the credit system. But at the same time it reduced the minimum purchase to eighty acres and cut the minimum price to $1.25 per acre.

These changes reflected the growing political power of the West. So did the concessions embodied in the Pre-Emption Act of 1841, which gave squatters first right to purchase land on which they had settled before it was surveyed and put up for general sale. Before then there had always been the danger, under the system of competitive bidding at an auction, that squatters would see their lands sold over their heads. But it was not until 1862 that the West obtained its heart's desire, the Homestead Act which made a free gift of 160 acres of public land to every settler.

Although the land laws were progressively liberalized, they did not, before 1862 at least, provide the easy access to the public domain that Jefferson had regarded as the best foundation for political and economic democracy. There was no limit to the amount of land that could be acquired, and no requirement that purchasers should actually settle on what they bought. This encouraged speculation and, in the Gulf States, enabled southern slave owners to build up great estates at the expense of small farmers. Moreover, since the average settler found the price of government land beyond his purse, he was forced to borrow from eastern bankers at high rates of interest. The consequence was that, in hard times, debt-ridden pioneers were frequently driven into a state of tenancy. Thus, while the West was settled predominantly by men who tilled their own acres, the pattern of ownership was not wholly democratic.

Broadly speaking, pioneers tended to migrate along lines of latitude. New Englanders, having moved into western New York in the 1790s and into northern Ohio the following decade, advanced from there into northern Indiana and Illinois and then to Michigan, Iowa, and Wisconsin. Further south, a second stream of migration followed a parallel course. This originated in Virginia,

North Carolina, and Kentucky, and flowed across the Ohio River to give southern Indiana and southern Illinois the character of a borderland between South and North. Finally, migration from the worn-out lands of Georgia and South Carolina ran due west into central Alabama and Mississippi before crossing the Mississippi into northern Louisiana and Arkansas. Yet within this broad tidal pattern there were crosscurrents. Future Confederate president Jefferson Davis's family, for example, headed southwest from Kentucky to Louisiana just before the War of 1812, but subsequently doubled back to settle in Mississippi. Moreover, during periods of depression there was a sizable reverse migration. Disappointed pioneers headed back to the East, their dreams of a more abundant life shattered.

Few of those who settled in the Mississippi Valley traveled long distances in the course of their migrations. Unlike those who took the Oregon Trail or trekked to Utah or California, emigrants to the Lake Plains and the Gulf Plains generally came from adjacent territories to the east. Moreover, settlers rarely stayed put for long. A typical frontier family was that of Abraham Lincoln. The future president's father, Thomas Lincoln, was a shiftless squatter who followed the frontier as it moved westward. Born in upcountry Virginia in 1778, he was taken four years later to Kentucky, where Abe was born in 1809. By 1816, the Lincolns had drifted to Indiana. There, they squatted for a year in a three-sided shack before moving into a typical log cabin, with a dirt floor, no windows or door, and a loft where young Abraham made his bed on a

*Frontier life disappointed many settlers. Major Walter Wilkey, shown here returning with his family to New England in 1839, had spent a "miserable half starved" year in Illinois.*

pile of leaves. This unpretentious dwelling was their only home for fifteen years before they pushed on to Illinois.

Loneliness, poverty, and a near-primitive existence were the lot of many frontiersmen, at least during the earliest stages of settlement. But in most settlements there was a steady advance, with frontier society passing through certain well-defined phases. These were described by the author of an emigrant guide book published in Boston in 1837:

> Generally, in all the western settlements, three classes, like the waves of the ocean, have rolled one after the other. First comes the pioneer, who depends for the subsistence of his family chiefly upon the natural growth of vegetation called the "range", and the proceeds of hunting. His implements of agriculture are rude, chiefly of his own make, and his efforts directed mostly to a crop of corn and a "truck patch".... He builds his cabin ... and occupies it until the range is somewhat subdued and hunting a little precarious; or, which is more frequently the case, till neighbors crowd round, roads, bridges and fields annoy him, and he lacks elbow room. The pre-emption law enables him to dispose of his cabin and corn-field to the next class of emigrant, and to employ his own figures, he "breaks for the high timbers, clears out for the New Purchase," or migrates to Arkansas or Texas to work the same process over.
>
> The next class of emigrants purchase the lands, add field to field, clear out the roads, throw rough bridges over the streams, put up hewn log houses, with glass windows and brick or stone chimneys, occasionally plant orchards, build mills, school houses, court houses, &c, and exhibit the pictures and forms of plain, frugal, civilized life.

Another wave rolls on. The men of capital and enterprise come. The "settler" is ready to sell out and take the advantage of the rise of property—push farther into the interior, and become himself a man of capital and enterprise in turn. The small village rises to a spacious town or city; substantial edifices of brick, extensive fields, orchards, gardens, colleges and churches are seen. Broadcloths, silks, leghorns, crapes and all the refinements, luxuries, elegancies, frivolities and fashions are in vogue. Thus wave after wave is rolling westward: the real *el dorado* is still farther on.

This process, repeated again and again in the years between 1815 and 1850, explains the rapid settlement of the Mississippi Valley. The speed of the frontier's advance had by midcentury transformed the political geography of the United States. In 1815, there had been eighteen states in the Union, only four of which (Kentucky, Tennessee, Ohio, and Louisiana) lay beyond the Appalachians. By 1850 there were thirty, fifteen of which were west of the mountains. Rapid settlement had also brought into existence two sections, whose economies and social orders diverged sharply. The simultaneous growth of the Cotton Kingdom with its stratified, slaveholding society, and of the more democratic Northwest with its diversified economy, added to the difficulty of welding the nation together.

## New Immigrants from Europe

To the strain of holding together a fast-expanding nation were added the problems of assimilating huge numbers of foreigners from a variety of European backgrounds. For the period which saw the settlement of the trans-Appalachian West was also one of mass immigration. This was a new experience for Americans. Until 1815, there were probably never more than 10,000 immigrants a year and usually many fewer. But hardly had the War of 1812 ended than an immigrant wave of unprecedented magni-

*Immigrants disembark at the Battery in New York Harbor. Artist Samuel Waugh portrays an uncommonly prosperous looking crowd of newcomers; most arrived with little more than their hopes.*

tude began. Slowly gathering momentum during the next three decades, it became a raging flood in the middle years of the century. In the decade of the 1820s—the first for which reliable statistics exist—the number of arrivals was 150,000, while in the 1830s it was just under 600,000. The 1840s brought a threefold increase to just over 1.7 million but this total was in turn dwarfed by the 2.6 million people who arrived in the 1850s. In each year between 1850 and 1854 the number of arrivals exceeded 300,000 and in 1854 itself it reached 428,000, a record which stood for two decades. By the standards of the late nineteenth century these figures are modest. But it should be remembered that the 5 million immigrants who came between 1815 and 1860 outnumbered the entire population of the United States in 1790. In proportion to population, the 3 million who arrived in the decade 1845–54 represented the greatest influx the nation would ever experience.

Nearly all the immigrants came from northern and western Europe. Over half of them had been born in the British Isles—2 million in Ireland and a further 750,000 in England, Wales, and Scotland. Germany contributed nearly 1 million and Switzerland, Norway, Sweden, and the Netherlands virtually all the rest.

Political and religious discontent had little part in this huge outflow. It is true that the outbreak of revolutions in Europe in 1830 and 1848 produced crops of exiles, but the numbers involved were not large. Nor did religious unrest provide much of a spur, except perhaps in Norway, where the exodus from the Stavanger region stemmed partly from the persecution of the Quakers, and in the Netherlands, where the 1846 exodus consisted of seceders from the Dutch Reformed Church. The real forces underlying the emigration movement were economic and applied to all nations involved. Essentially it was the pressure of rising population, coinciding with the transformation of the old economic order, that dislodged people from their homes. In England and Germany, the Industrial Revolution destroyed the old system of domestic manufacture and threw great numbers of artisans out of work. At the same time, the rise of large-scale scientific farming spelled the end of the old communal system of agriculture and displaced a large proportion of the rural population; many of these erstwhile farmers began to look overseas.

Nowhere was economic change better calculated to produce emigration than in Ireland. It was the most densely populated country in Europe, and the system of land ownership kept the mass of the peasantry in a state of chronic poverty. The gradual deterioration of Irish agriculture after 1815 swelled the tide of departures for America. But after the potato famine of 1845–49, the floodgates were opened. The failure of the potato crop caused 1 million deaths from starvation and fever, and convinced many of the survivors that it was futile to remain

THE CAUSES OF EMIGRATION IN IRELAND.

*Barraged by debt collectors and threatened by the bailiff, this Irishman has good cause to emigrate. His son points toward America while his wife hangs her head in despair.*

longer in Ireland. Despair seized not only the laborer and the tenant farmer but the small farm-owner also. Thus, even when the panic-stricken flight from hunger was over, the exodus continued. The 1.5 million Irishmen who crossed the Atlantic in the next decade were drawn from all classes, though the great majority were extremely poor.

The typical German emigrant of the period was the victim neither of oppression nor of want. He, like emigrants from other parts of Europe, was simply a casualty of economic and social dislocation. That German emigration reached its peak immediately after the 1848 revolutions was purely a coincidence. The great mass of German emigrants came, as one historian put it, from "classes which had been little concerned with politics and with revolution not at all." They came from those parts of Germany—Wurttemberg, Baden, Bavaria—where small agricultural holdings prevailed but where, as in Ireland, the consolidation of farms was squeezing out the small man. These difficulties, as well as the repeated crop failures of the 1840s and 1850s which ruined count-

less small farmers, caused many to leave for America. But even greater numbers decided not to wait until disaster struck. They preferred to emigrate while they could still get enough from the sale of their property to enable them to start afresh in America. They went, that is to say, in order to better their condition, but also because they were fearful of losing what they had if they stayed put. This was the situation of a great many emigrants during this period, not alone from Germany, but from England and Scandinavia also.

## Why the Immigrants Came

Yet the problems caused by population growth and economic change would not, by themselves, have sent tidal waves of discontented people across the Atlantic. There were also a heightened awareness of American opportunity, a lessening of restraints on emigration, and an increase in the facilities for reaching the New World. Popular knowledge of the United States grew rapidly in the early decades of the nineteenth century. This was the product of rising educational standards, cheap books and newspapers, and a vast improvement in postal services. Travel accounts like Morris Birkbeck's *Letters from Illinois* (1818) and the Norwegian Ole Rynning's *True Account of America* (1838) were two among the many which helped dispel the common man's ignorance of American conditions. Emigrant guidebooks appeared by the score, providing detailed information about wages,

*Immigrants brought with them some well-known national institutions. The Germans, for example, introduced the convivial beer garden to America. Below: Guidebooks informed—and warned—potential European emigrants about many aspects of life in America. They helped smooth the transition to a totally different society.*

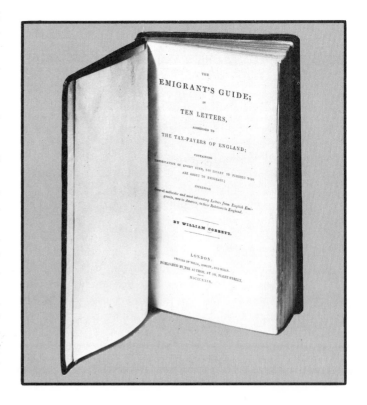

prices, crops, soils, and climates in different parts of the Union. Yet the most important source of information to the would-be emigrant, as well as the most reliable, was the "America-letter," a communication written by a friend or relative who had emigrated earlier. These personal missives generally spoke in glowing terms of the advantages America offered. They thus contributed much to emigration fever, while the advice and information they contained probably helped to lessen fears of the unknown.

Whether the desire to move could be acted upon depended, however, upon the reaction of governments to a prospective loss of population. Ever since the middle of the seventeenth century, emigration had been officially frowned upon. Every government in Europe had endorsed the mercantilist doctrine that the wealth of a nation was proportionate to its population. They had seen emigration simply as a drain on national strength. Accordingly, they had either forbidden emigration altogether or had hampered it in various ways. But once it became apparent how fast the European population was increasing, there was a change in official attitudes. The specter of overpopulation was conjured up in 1798 by the English clergyman-economist Thomas Malthus, who argued that the rise in numbers would always tend to outstrip the means of subsistence. Governments grew increasingly ready to see emigration, not as a national evil, but as a remedy for pauperism and a safety valve for discontent. After 1815, one government after another either simplified or abolished the legal restraints that had surrounded emigration. For the first time, subjects of European monarchs were free to leave their native lands.

Increasing freedom to move coincided with an expansion of the means to do so. For the European poor, the cost of a transatlantic voyage had been prohibitive. But in the decades after 1815, the growth of transatlantic commerce brought about a great expansion in cheap transportation facilities. The merchant vessels which transported raw materials to Europe from the United States and Canada were always short of return freights, because European goods occupied less cargo space than the timber, cotton, and tobacco carried eastward. They were therefore glad of the emigrant trade, which offered fat profits and involved little outlay. It cost very little to construct temporary wooden berths in the steerage and supply emigrants with the meager rations of food and water demanded by law. The result was that the emigrant trade became a highly organized business. It tended increasingly to become concentrated at the larger ports of departure, such as Liverpool, Le Havre, Bremen, and Hamburg. Passenger brokers made a practice of chartering the between-decks of merchant vessels. To ensure full complements, they established networks of agencies to tap the emigrant stream at its different sources. The resulting competition reduced steerage fares to about $20, and in Irish ports they were often lower still. This

was still more than the poorest classes could afford, but many of them were nevertheless able to reach America because of the development of the prepaid passage system. A sizable proportion of the great total—perhaps as much as one-half—owed its ability to emigrate to the receipt of tickets or money sent by relatives who had emigrated earlier.

Cheap though the Atlantic crossing had now become, it remained a harsh and nauseating ordeal. Until the 1860s, when steam took the place of sail, the journey took an average of six weeks, though in bad weather it might last as long as three months. The emigrant carriers of the period were a varied lot, ranging from frequently unseaworthy British timber ships and sturdy German freighters to well-built and handsome American packet ships. The one feature that all emigrant sailing ships had in common was that, having been built primarily for freight, they were ill suited to the carriage of passengers. The steerage quarters on a typical emigrant ship consisted of a single, undivided compartment about 150 feet long by 35 feet wide. Light and ventilation were poor, sanitary facilities primitive, and comfort nonexistent. In these dark and fetid surroundings, hundreds of emigrants of all ages and both sexes were huddled together like cattle for weeks at a time. They ate coarse and badly cooked food, and often wallowed in filth and vomit. Small wonder that infectious diseases were common and that, having once broken out, they spread like wildfire. Ship fever, measles, and smallpox were frequent visitors, and whenever typhus or cholera raged at the ports of embarkation, they were invariably carried into the steerage and could be counted on to exact a horrifying toll at sea. There were scores of deaths on emigrant ships during a cholera outbreak in 1832, and hundreds during another in 1853–54. But the worst horrors occurred in 1847, when more than 17,000 emigrants, mainly Irish, died from ship fever during the voyage or shortly after landing. An even larger number arrived in the New World so enfeebled as to require hospital treatment.

In response to the public outcry at these scandals, governments on both sides of the Atlantic repeatedly amended the laws regulating steerage conditions. But they were reluctant to make the regulations too stringent, lest the result should be a rise in fares which would act as a brake on emigration. In any case, the Passenger Acts were difficult to enforce and many of their provisions were dead letters. There was little improvement until steam replaced sail and medical science revealed more about the causes and control of epidemic disease.

Exploitation and hardship awaited the emigrant not only during the crossing but at every stage of his journey. At the port of departure, harpies and swindlers infested the docks and preyed upon the unsuspecting. Then, the moment he set foot in America, the newcomer was pounced upon by an army of runners, ticket sellers, employment agents, and boardinghouse touts—many of them out to fleece him. A New York investigating committee was shocked in 1846 at the amount of fraud and deception practiced upon newly arrived immigrants, mostly by their own countrymen. It found "the German preying upon the German—the Irish upon the Irish— the English upon the English." True, the various immigrant benevolent organizations did what they could to protect and shelter their own nationals, but they lacked the necessary resources and authority. Not until 1855, when the state of New York established a controlled immigrant depot at Castle Garden, near the Battery at the tip of Manhattan, were new arrivals given some degree of protection. Even then, they were not entirely free from exploitation. But at least the grosser forms of abuse were eliminated.

## Patterns of Settlement

Nearly all the immigrants landed in New York and in other northern ports, and it was in the Northeast that the overwhelming majority settled. Even those who landed at New Orleans tended to take a steamboat up the Mississippi to the free states. The hot climate of the South repelled immigrants, as did the presence of Negro slaves. But the main reason why the section was so largely shunned was that it could not offer jobs so readily as the North, nor provide the kind of farmland immigrants were looking for. Hence the immigrants were increasingly concentrated in two main areas: the Eastern Seaboard cities from Boston to Baltimore, and the upper Middle West, especially Illinois, Wisconsin, Iowa, and Minnesota.

Those with industrial skills tended to congregate in the American centers of their trades—coal miners in Pennsylvania, lead miners in Illinois, potters in Ohio, textile workers in New England. Tailors, carpenters, and other craftsmen made for the cities, especially the larger ones, where employment was most readily obtained. Agricultural skills, however, could be transported only to regions where farming conditions were not too dissimilar from those in Europe. This meant that immigrant farmers rarely took up land on the frontier, where novel farming techniques were necessary and familiarity with an ax and a rifle were essential to survival. The usual practice was for immigrant farmers to take over improved farms whose owners were ready to move further west.

The proportion of immigrants who took up farming varied greatly from one ethnic group to another. Agriculture was perhaps most popular with Norwegians and Swedes. They settled so thickly in parts of Wisconsin and Minnesota that the region acquired a pronounced Scandinavian flavor. A high percentage of the Dutch, too, were drawn to farming, especially in Michigan and Iowa.

The journey to a new land marked the start of a great adventure. Above left: A crowded shipload of emigrants bid farewell to Ireland. Above

right: *On his voyage to America in 1824, Joseph W. Gear sketched this scene of breakfast for steerage passengers. Below left: This woodcut shows immigrants landing in New York. Below right: A newly arrived Irish family receives a mock salute from a shoe-shine boy.*

*This primitive painting shows Swedish farmers at work in the fields. Along with other Scandinavian immigrants, the Swedes settled in considerable numbers in Minnesota and Wisconsin.*

The Germans, however, were more variously distributed. Very large numbers became farmers in the Middle West, particularly in Ohio, Illinois, Wisconsin, and Iowa, as well as in Texas. But perhaps as many Germans settled in the towns and cities. Some small towns were almost wholly German. Belleville, Illinois, in the 1850s had a German mayor, a German majority on the city council, and three German newspapers; even the local Negroes spoke German. Still more robustly German were Hermann, Missouri, and Fredericksburg, Texas. But the heaviest German concentrations were in big cities such as Milwaukee, Cincinnati, St Louis, and New York, in each of which there were wholly Germanized sections. In Cincinnati's "Over the Rhine" or New York's *Kleindeutschland*, the English language was rarely heard. Here, every business was run by Germans and every church, school, and restaurant was German. But the most characteristic and widespread German institution was the beer garden. Here, on holidays, beer flowed plentifully to the lusty accompaniment of German singing. But it would be wrong to paint too rosy a picture of life in a German urban ghetto. An appreciable number of Germans lived, for a time at least, in conditions of extreme squalor. A New York legislative committee in 1857 came across a row of wooden tenements occupied by German immigrants who subsisted on offal and scraps and lived "in almost fabulous gregari-

ousness." They were surrounded by piles of filthy rags, the bones of dead animals, and "noisome collections of every kind . . . reeking with pestiferous smells."

But it was among the Irish that urban concentration was most marked. This fact sometimes puzzled contemporaries. They found it strange that a group which was overwhelmingly of rural origin, and which in the old country had been so attached to the soil, should so rarely have settled on the land in the United States. But the explanation was not hard to find. The Irish lacked both the experience and the capital to become farmers, in the West or elsewhere. They knew little of agriculture except how to raise potatoes, and the potato famine had left them disenchanted with the land. Moreover, as a sociable people, accustomed at home to life in close-knit communities, they were repelled by the loneliness of farm life. From time to time, efforts were made to colonize large bodies of Irishmen on western land. But there was strong opposition from eastern members of the Roman Catholic hierarchy. The bishops feared that the dispersal of the

Irish into regions where the consolations of religion were hard to obtain would lead to a loss of faith.

For these reasons, and because they were too poverty-stricken and too debilitated to do anything else, most of the Irish congregated in the eastern cities, especially New York, Boston, and Philadelphia. Some made their way to the factory towns of New England, some to Mississippi river towns, others to the growing cities of the West like Chicago and St Louis. Wherever they settled, they became slum dwellers, living in garrets, cellars, tenements, old warehouses, and flimsy one-room shacks. Thus, to the terrors of the Atlantic crossing were now added the hardships of urban life in America. The squalid, dilapidated, and densely populated quarters in which the Irish lived proved excellent breeding grounds for disease. Sections like Boston's North End and New York's Five Points became notorious for epidemics and heavy mortality rates.

In the land of opportunity, moreover, the Irish became not only slum dwellers but a depressed proletariat. They possessed fewer skills and smaller resources than any immigrant group of the pre-Civil War period. They also encountered more prejudice. By the 1840s, the notice ''No Irish Need Apply'' was a familiar one to newcomers scanning the New York or Boston job advertisement columns. The Irish had thus to depend heavily on the

lowest and the most menial occupations; they became laborers, carters, porters, and waiters—or more commonly still, domestic servants. Within a short time the Irish had won a virtual monopoly of unskilled jobs in American cities. They were also increasingly prominent in construction work. Finding employment in the cities uncertain and sporadic, they frequently ventured forth to take on the back-breaking work of digging canals and building railroads. They found conditions in the construction camps harsh, and all too often they were cheated of their wages by unscrupulous contractors. Gradually, the Irish began to infiltrate into industry, especially in the New England textile mills (where they replaced native-born farm girls) or in the Pennsylvania coalfields. But on the eve of the Civil War they were still at the bottom of the occupational ladder.

By midcentury, the economic benefits to the nation of mass immigration were everywhere apparent. As well as contributing to the rapid settlement of the Mississippi Valley, it had hastened the construction of a transportation network and the growth of industry. Without the

*Heavy immigration led to congestion, squalor, and crime in the large eastern cities. Five Points, in the lower east side of Manhattan, was a crowded ghetto with a high murder rate.*

Brown Brothers

79

reservoir of cheap labor provided by immigration, the highways, canals, and railroads would have been delayed. And without the technological skills and know-how of immigrant craftsmen, artisans, operatives, and managers, the initial phases of American industrialization would have been more protracted.

## Nativist Fears and Resentment

Yet some Americans were alarmed by the rising tide of immigration. By the 1850s foreigners made up almost half the population of New York, Chicago, Cincinnati, Milwaukee, Detroit, and San Francisco. The proportion was not much less in New Orleans, Baltimore, and Boston; in St Louis, immigrants outnumbered the native-born by almost two to one. But it was not the growing numbers of immigrants that produced misgivings, or even the fact that they were so heavily concentrated in the larger cities. It was rather the feeling that the economic stimulus resulting from immigration had been purchased at the cost of social unity.

Americans had always prided themselves on their freedom from European social evils. Paupers and beggars had been virtually unknown, crime only a minor problem. But the immigrant tide brought with it worrying problems of pauperism and criminality. Especially in the eastern cities, there was much resentment at the burden placed on public funds and private charity by the alien poor. In Boston, the president of the Society for the Prevention of Pauperism complained in 1849 that two-thirds of the paupers in Massachusetts were foreigners, most of them Irish. Five years later, the New York Association for Improving the Condition of the Poor published figures that revealed just how much the foreign-born poor were costing the New York taxpayer. Of the immigrants who had arrived in New York since 1847, no fewer than 617,000 had received state or municipal assistance, at a total cost of about $2.3 million. Providing relief for these unfortunates had become the heaviest charge on the public purse, and in the middle 1850s there were clamorous demands for measures to check the influx of paupers.

Crime statistics showed a similar disproportion between immigrants and the native-born. In 1850, there were three times as many foreign-born inmates of the New York state prisons as there were natives. New York City police reports told the same story, and also revealed that the Irish came into conflict with the law far more often than any other group. In a typical quarter, May-July 1858, only 2,690 of the 17,328 persons arrested were natives of the United States. The Irish accounted for 10,477, the Germans for 1,621, the English for 666, and a variety of other foreign-born groups for the remaining 1,874. The statistics were misleading in that most of the arrests were for relatively minor offences, especially drunkenness and disorderly conduct. But this was not generally appreciated, and the impression left on most minds by such reports was one of immigrant, and especially Irish, criminality.

What swelled the volume of protest at the burden of foreign destitution and lawlessness was the belief that it stemmed largely from the European practice of systematically shipping undesirables across the Atlantic. A Congressional committee complained in 1856 that European communities were making the United States the "receptacle for the dregs and off-scourings of their population . . . thus relieving themselves of the burden of pauperism and crime." The allegation was not altogether groundless. At different times, local authorities in Britain, Belgium, Switzerland, and Germany all used public funds to send away lawbreakers and the unemployable. But reports of European dumping were absurdly exaggerated. In no year did the numbers sent out at public expense account for more than a minute fraction of the total immigration. The vast majority of those who got into trouble with the law in the United States had not had criminal records in Europe. Nor had the bulk of those who created a relief problem in America been paupers at home (in the sense that they had been dependent for their livelihood on public charity).

Americans were also disturbed at the political role of the foreign-born. They saw how many of the newcomers were ill-educated or illiterate, how ignorant most of them were of American institutions, and yet how, in some places, they had become numerous enough to hold the balance of political power. They saw, too, how the entry of immigrants into politics resulted in electoral violence and voting frauds. Native-born voters were barred from the polls by organized mobs of Irish laborers; immigrants cast ballots before they were qualified to do so; and false testimony became commonplace in naturalization proceedings. Could republican freedom and government survive such malpractices? Not that corruption was the only threat which immigrants appeared to pose to the American political system. There was even the possibility of revolution. By opening its doors to political refugees, the United States had acquired an assortment of turbulent spirits who, having failed to revolutionize their native countries, intended to pursue the same object in this adopted land. Such, at least, was the conclusion many Americans drew from the radical program put forward by some of the German immigrants after 1848.

Some Americans were also concerned at the extent to which immigrants continued to take an active interest in Old World causes. The formation of such Irish-American organizations as the Fenian Brotherhood, which carried on a strenuous agitation in favor of Irish independence, attracted hostile comment from nativists. So did the activities of those whose preoccupation with German politics was so intense as to give the impression that they saw America merely as a base from which to plan the next revolution in Germany. Such transatlantic attachments, nativists argued, were inconsistent with the obligations of American citizenship. Immigrants should give America their undivided allegiance and refrain from agitation which might involve her in war with European powers.

## Anti-Catholicism and the Know-Nothings

Yet it was anti-Catholicism which contributed most to suspicion of immigrants. Until the 1830s, the United States could be described as a Protestant country, but most of the immigrants from Ireland and many of those from Germany were Catholics. The growth of the population led to a corresponding increase in the number of Catholic priests and bishops, convents and monasteries, schools and colleges. This alarmed many of the native-born and led to a revival of the anti-Catholicism that had been rife in colonial America. Unlike earlier expressions of hostility toward Rome, however, this new agitation had little to do with differences over dogma or ritual. It arose rather from the fear that the Catholic influx threatened American political institutions. Protestants saw the Catholic church less as a religious than a political institution, closely allied with despotism and tyranny in Europe and opposed to political liberty in America. Some of the excited anti-Catholics, like Samuel F. B. Morse, the portrait painter and inventor of the telegraph, believed in the existence of a popish plot to destroy American Protestantism and subvert free government in the young republic. Morse's pamphlet, *A Foreign Conspiracy against the Liberties of the United States*, published in 1834, pointed to the Catholic influx as proof of the Pope's nefarious designs and urged Americans to unite to thwart them.

In the same year occurred the first of a number of mob attacks against Catholic institutions—the burning of the Ursuline Convent at Charlestown, Massachusetts. This was the signal for a flood of sensational literature purporting to describe the immorality prevailing in convents and among the priesthood. The most notorious and the most widely read of these fabrications was Maria Monk's *Awful Disclosures of the Hôtel Dieu Nunnery at Montreal* (1836), though its success told more about the appeal of pornography than the strength of popular anti-Catholicism. Fears of Romanism persisted nonetheless and were greatly increased by the school controversy in New York City in the early 1840s. Catholic opposition to the use of the King James version of the Bible in the public schools, and Catholic demands for a share in the state school fund, were bitterly criticized by Protestants; it seemed to them blasphemous, divisive, and un-American. What further incensed Protestants was the action of Bishop John Hughes of New York, who ran a separate Catholic ticket

*This Know-Nothing cartoon lampoons the German and Irish in America. Many undesirable features of American society—like drunkenness—were laid at the door of immigrant groups.*

in the 1841 elections. They denounced this step as a violation of the principle of the separation of church and state. The New York agitation soon died away, only for a similar controversy to erupt in Philadelphia. In 1844, there were serious anti-Catholic riots which resulted in the destruction of several churches and the death and wounding of individual Catholics.

The founding of the Native American party in 1845 marked the entry of antiforeignism into politics. But political nativism did not begin to attract widespread support until the 1850s, when a group of secret nativist societies united to form a national organization, the Order of the Star-Spangled Banner. This, too, was a secret society, and because members refused to answer questions about its activities, they were nicknamed Know-Nothings. The aims of Know-Nothingism became clear, however, in 1854 with the appearance of the American party, whose slogan was "America for Americans." This rallying-cry did not mean that Know-Nothings wished to put a stop to immigration. The only immigrants they wanted to exclude were paupers and criminals. But they felt that those who were allowed to enter the United States should not enter politics until they had become Americanized. Aliens, they said, should not be allowed to vote or hold office, and the residential qualification for naturalization should be extended from five to twenty-one years.

Political nativism reached its height in the middle 1850s, when Know-Nothingism, in the guise of the American party, won spectacular victories in local elections and temporarily controlled six states. But except in Massachusetts, where the ballot was withheld from immigrants for a period of two years after naturalization and foreign

*An American youth, challenging the arrival of the Pope, claims he "knows nothing" but the Bible. Brother Jonathan, the predecessor of Uncle Sam, warns the delegation that Americans will not be receptive to conversion.*

militia companies were ordered to disband, the Know-Nothing program failed to reach the statute book. The reason was that, once in office, disagreement over the slavery issue shattered party unity. After the 1856 presidential election, in which the Know-Nothing candidate, Millard Fillmore, carried only one state, the party disintegrated. By 1860 the immigrant issue was dead.

Over the country as a whole, nativism had never been more than a minority creed. Most Americans had held firmly to the belief that their country was destined to be a refuge for the oppressed of the Old World. They had remained confident of its ability to assimilate the throngs of newcomers. Faith in these traditional ideals was never more eloquently expressed than during the years when the immigrant tide was rising highest. Theodore Parker urged that the New World should be "the Asylum of Humanity for this century as for the seventeenth," while to Emerson the mixing of nationalities which immigra-

tion produced would result in a new and superior race. It was Herman Melville who produced the most high-minded refutation of nativist ideals. In his autobiographical novel, *Redburn*, published in 1849, he described the emotions he experienced while watching German emigrants embark at Liverpool for America:

> There is something in the contemplation of the mode in which America has been settled that, in a noble breast, should forever extinguish the prejudices of national dislikes. . . . Settled by the people of all nations, all nations may claim her for their own. . . . We are not a narrow tribe of men. . . . No, our blood is as the flood of the Amazon, made up of a thousand noble currents all pouring into one. We are not a nation, so much as a world. . . .

Yet within a few years it was to be evident that the United States was in reality a nation as well as a world. When the Civil War broke out in 1861, immigrants sprang to the defense of the Union with as much speed and enthusiasm as the native-born. The fierce American nationalism which the foreign-born displayed in the Union's hour of need proved that Melville's hopes for America's future had been more soundly based than the fears of the nativists.

*Chapter 4*

# A SEARCH FOR BETTERMENT

*Tocqueville observed that "the ideas of progress and of the indefinite perfectibility of the human race belong to democratic ages. Democratic nations care but little for what has been, but they are haunted by visions of what will be." In education, religion, and social reform the aim was the same— the improvement of man. With the founding of public schools went a new emphasis on practical instruction to enable children to serve a useful role in later life. At camp meetings and in churches, powerful orators won a wide following, while idealists of many stripes engaged in utopian experiments. And in the cities, social reformers rallied to the plight of the less fortunate. The conscience of America was stirring.*

# Americans in School

Throughout the Western world of the nineteenth century there was a boom in education. Governments pushed it. So did religious groups. Rich men gave money for it. There was a new crop of professional educators, eager to see their theories realized in fresh or improved types of school or college. The spokesmen for education did not always agree with one another. In some countries, especially in Europe, there was a considerable emphasis on the dangers of extending education too widely. Conservatives were anxious to ensure that education should be used to train people for limited tasks, and to make them accept their place in life. In the words of the *Encyclopædia Britannica* (3rd edition, 1797): "Let the youth who is born to pass his days in a humble station be carefully taught to consider honest industry as one of the first of virtues. Teach him contentment with his lot." Nevertheless, most Western nations felt that education was important for cementing national unity. In the early nineteenth century, for instance, France and Prussia began to develop complete, centralized systems of schooling. Each stressed the history, literature, and culture of its own fatherland. In general, too, educators believed that children should be taught moral values, to make them better citizens.

These broad concerns were given an added weight in the United States. With independence came a flood of writing and speechmaking about the desired shape of the new nation. Education was allotted a central role. A federal, republican democracy was a new conception, derided or dreaded by many people in Europe. The United States must therefore, it was said, create new forms of education. European models would not do. The American citizen must be taught to think like an American—all the more vital if he happened to be of recently arrived immigrant stock. Since there was no aristocracy in the United States, leaders would have to be produced in the schools and colleges of the nation. Political health would depend on a literate, sophisticated electorate.

It was thus no accident that every prominent American of the generation of the Founding Fathers put education high on his list of priorities. For James Madison: "A popular government without popular information or the means of acquiring it, is but a prologue to a farce or a tragedy." So said John Jay: "Knowledge is the soul of the republic and nothing should be left undone to afford all ranks of the people a means of attaining it." So wrote Thomas Jefferson, from Paris, to his old mentor Justice Wythe: "Preach a crusade against ignorance; establish and improve the law for educating the common people." President Washington said, in his first message to Congress: "Knowledge is, in every country, the surest basis of public happiness. In one in which the . . . government receives impressions as immediately from the sense of the community as ours, it is . . . essential." Washington was keenly interested in a move to establish a national university, located in the nation's capital. Like Jefferson, he thought Americans who went abroad for their education were exposed to harmful foreign attitudes. If young men could be brought together from all parts of the country, the experience would help to strengthen the Union.

The lexicographer Noah Webster had the same idea. Webster was among the first to grasp what education could do to weld together the new nation. His dictionary was called *An American Dictionary of the English Language*. "Nothing but the establishment of schools and some uniformity in the use of books," he claimed, "can annihilate differences in speaking and preserve the purity of the American tongue." Webster's *Speller*—the ever-famous "Blue-Backed Speller"—taught a common spelling and pronunciation suitable for a unified and democratic people. His many *Readers* familiarized children all over the Union with a common stock of inspirational stories, many drawn from American experience.

*The title page of the first volume of Webster's* An American Dictionary of the English Language *as it appeared in 1828. His aim was to standardize American usage.*

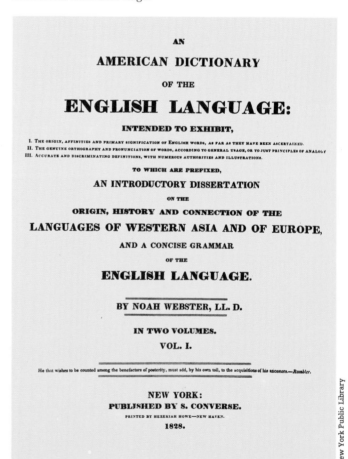

AN

**AMERICAN DICTIONARY**

OF THE

**ENGLISH LANGUAGE:**

**INTENDED TO EXHIBIT,**

I. The origin, affinities and primary signification of English words, as far as they have been ascertained.
II. The genuine orthography and pronunciation of words, according to general usage, or to just principles of analogy.
III. Accurate and discriminating definitions, with numerous authorities and illustrations.

TO WHICH ARE PREFIXED,

**AN INTRODUCTORY DISSERTATION**

ON THE

**ORIGIN, HISTORY AND CONNECTION OF THE**

**LANGUAGES OF WESTERN ASIA AND OF EUROPE,**

AND A CONCISE GRAMMAR

OF THE

**ENGLISH LANGUAGE.**

**BY NOAH WEBSTER, LL. D.**

**IN TWO VOLUMES.**

**VOL. I.**

He that wishes to be counted among the benefactors of posterity, must add, by his own toil, to the acquisitions of his ancestors.—*Rambler.*

**NEW YORK:**
**PUBLISHED BY S. CONVERSE.**
PRINTED BY HEZEKIAH HOWE—NEW HAVEN.
**1828.**

*Above: Grammars, spellers, and readers used by schoolchildren of the mid-nineteenth century. Right: Horace Mann began his career in politics but turned his interests in 1837 to the education of the young. He fought for the idea of public schools and good teachers.*

Nor was Webster alone in campaigning to make the schools the nurseries of nationalism. Dr Benjamin Rush of Philadelphia, the best-known physician of his day and a signer of the Declaration of Independence, thought every child should be made into a "republican machine." The role of education in encouraging political harmony was the theme, too, of most of the essays submitted to the American Philosophical Society for a prize contest in 1797. Alarm at the spread of southern and western sectionalism in the next decades reinforced the plea for education as an Americanizing cement. This drive found ever more urgent expression in the flow of *Readers* and *Spellers* which poured out of the busy pens of the McGuffey brothers. It featured in the writings of educators like Horace Mann in Massachusetts and Henry Barnard in Connecticut. Mann indeed treated education

as a kind of American miracle drug, capable of curing every possible ailment and indispensable to the nation's healthy survival. As he announced in his 1848 report to the Massachusetts board of education:

> According to the European theory, men are divided into classes, some to toil and earn, others to seize and enjoy. According to the Massachusetts theory all are to have an equal chance for earning and equal security in the enjoyment of what they earn. The European theory is blind to what constitutes the highest glory as well as the highest duty of a State. . . . Education, beyond all other devices of human origin, is the great equalizer of the conditions of men, the balance wheel of the social machinery. It does better than to disarm the poor of their hostility toward the rich, it prevents their being poor.

## A Boom in "Practical" Education

Mixed in with these fairly lofty functions, American education was also expected to be *practical*. Even before the Revolution some colonists regarded traditional education as a waste of time. What use were Greek and Latin, rhetoric and philosophy, for youngsters who needed to be able to turn their hands to other, more pressing tasks? There was work to be done if each new frontier community was to survive; the nourishment of the mind or the sensibility could come later. This was well stated by John Adams, writing to his wife during the Revolution: "I must study politics and war that my sons may have liberty to study mathematics and philosophy. My sons ought to study mathematics and philosophy, geography, natural history and naval architecture, navigation, commerce and agriculture, in order to give their children a right to study painting, poetry, music, architecture, statuary, tapestry and porcelain."

One result was that the Latin or grammar schools, the best secondary institutions of the colonial era, began to give way to "academies," dedicated to preparing students for life in America rather than in the Middle Ages. The first successful academy in America had been founded by Benjamin Franklin in Philadelphia, as early as 1751. New England, however, fixed the pattern of the academy which was to spread through the country with such rapidity. Two famous examples were Phillips Andover and Phillips Exeter, begun during the revolutionary war. The new academies did not dispense with Latin and Greek, but they did add instruction in more practical subjects. Equally important was the aim, which they shared with the colleges of the day. Phillips Andover, for example, was committed to "instructing Youth not only in English and Latin Grammar, Writing, Arithmetic, and those sciences wherein they are commonly taught; but

more especially to learn them the great end and business of living. . . . It is again declared that the . . . principal object of this institution is the promotion of true piety and virtue."

This somewhat more realistic secondary education speedily caught on, and soon swept through all the original thirteen states. By 1850 there were about 1,000 academies in New England, 1,600 in the Middle Atlantic States, and no less than 2,640 in the South. Only in the newer states of the Old Northwest did high schools outstrip academies in number and authority. Some of these schools dressed their pupils in uniform and gave them military training; examples include Alden Partridge's academy at Norwich, Vermont (founded in 1819), the Virginia Military Institute at Lexington (1839), and the Citadel in Charleston, South Carolina (1843). Some, in size and quality, were not very different from the smaller colleges of the day. They came in every variety, ranging from excellent to abysmal. The better ones prospered. The bad or unlucky ones often lasted only a few years.

Similar things could be said of American colleges. Nine had been founded during the colonial period—more than in contemporary Britain. By the time of the Civil War about 500 existed, though even more had had to close down, being unable to survive the fierce competition for students and their fees. The main reason for this remarkable growth is the determination of religious denominations to plant their flags in each state and on each successive frontier. Leading citizens in America's small towns, wanting to "boost" their attractions, met the college founders halfway by putting up money and offering land. Of the successful establishments in 1860, the Presbyterians could boast 49 colleges, the Methodists 34, the Baptists 25, the Congregationalists 21, and the Episcopalians 11; while the Catholics had by that time founded 14 colleges and theological seminaries, among them St Louis University in Missouri and Fordham in New York City.

The picture would thus appear to be of expansion and progress in every branch of education. In addition to the hundreds of academies, seminaries, and colleges, men like Mann and Barnard were winning the battle for the principle of universal free "common" or "grade" schooling. They insisted that a basic education on this level was the birthright of every American child. By the 1820s, church denominations were active in starting Sunday schools, with the notion that every child in the congregation should be given a grounding in religious education. In the same decade, adult education began to flower, in the shape of the "Lyceum" movement pioneered in the United States by Josiah Holbrook. His American Lyceum started as a sort of mutual-aid organization. It evolved into a lecture circuit, or in the words of Ralph Waldo Emerson "a pulpit which makes all other pulpits ineffectual." The Lyceum concept enabled local communities throughout the country to see and hear such platform

*Above: A daguerreotype of a class at the Emerson School in Boston around 1850. Below: A humorous look at adult education. A Lyceum lecturer in meteorology holds forth at Clinton Hall, New York.*

oracles as the "Great American Preacher" Theodore Parker; the Harvard zoologist Louis Agassiz; the eloquent reformer Senator Charles Sumner; the courageous abolitionist Wendell Phillips; the temperance advocate John Gough; Bayard Taylor who all but invented the travelogue and enchanted audiences with his accounts of romantic places and exotic civilizations; and of course Emerson himself. In American cities there were, as well, a growing number of places like the Franklin Institute of Philadelphia which offered practical instruction in science and commerce for young workmen and businessmen. They included the Lowell Institute in Boston, the Peabody in Baltimore, and the Cooper Union in New York. This was started in the 1850s by the iron-manufacturer and philanthropist Peter Cooper, and gave classes not only in engineering and architecture but in the fine arts.

Even more important in popular education was the role of libraries—at first semipublic ones maintained by subscriptions, like the Society Library in New York, the Redwood in Newport, and the Athenæum in Boston. The free public library was born in New England at the beginning of the century, though another half century went by before the founding of Boston's magnificent public library. The public library idea spread so rapidly that by 1860 Americans had access to over 10,000.

A writer of the 1840s, the Virginian George Tucker, included two other agencies which he thought helped to educate people. The first was the clergy, numbering over 20,000 at the 1840 census. The second was "the periodical press." By 1840 there were in the United States about 1,500 newspapers—dailies, weeklies, and twice- or thrice-weeklies. The press, said Tucker, "keeps every part of the country informed of all that has occurred in every other": science and medicine, art and amusement, politics and

trade, romance and crime. A joke told in one city, or an argument developed in Congress, was "in little more than a week, repeated in every town in the United States." Tucker believed that "such a diffusion of intelligence and information has never existed in any other country."

## Two Surprising Shortcomings

But the picture is not quite as glowing or as clearcut as it is sometimes painted. One apparent paradox is that the United States, relying so heavily on education to foster national unity, never developed a national system or a national philosophy of education. Schools were, and remained, state and local affairs, and even the states found it almost impossible to impose any pattern or standard on rural academies or city schools. The national government made substantial grants of public land—an eventual total of nearly 150 million acres—to finance both elementary and higher education. But it never tried to tie strings to these grants. The how, what, and where of teaching remained a matter for state legislatures or local school boards. George Washington's dream of a national university faded away in the early nineteenth century into the realm of might-have-beens. The nearest thing to a national educational institution was the US Military Academy, which started life in 1802 and began to be significant in about 1820. The US Naval Academy at Annapolis, a counterpart to the army's West Point, did not start until 1845, and was just beginning to make itself felt when the Civil War came. This is not to say that American education was ruined by the lack of federal control, but simply that there was no central direction.

A more intriguing surprise is that, despite Americans' near-obsession with education, they made few new contributions to educational theory or practice. Though in many ways less democratic and less flexible than the United States, it was Europe that generated the fresh ideas. The roots of the Lyceum lay in England. England launched the "Lancasterian" or "monitorial" method of teaching, by which the older pupils looked after the younger ones. The "normal school," now known as a teacher training college, was a mixture of French theory and Swiss and German practice. The term normal school was coined by the French minister of education, Victor Cousin, to describe the teacher training institutions he admired in Prussia and other German states. American educational pioneers, including Horace Mann, went to Europe to inspect such schemes, and urged that they be tried out in the United States. As early as the 1820s, to be sure, Samuel Hall had set up a kind of training college in Vermont. But the full movement for teacher training came twenty years later.

The idea of the kindergarten ("children's garden") likewise arose in Europe. The underlying notion, that children should be allowed to develop their own personalities instead of having information pounded into them, was explained by the Frenchman Jean Jacques Rousseau, even before the American Revolution. A great Swiss educator, Heinrich Pestalozzi, transformed Rousseau's theories into reality. Educators from elsewhere in Europe and from America soon arrived to study Pestalozzi's cheerful, informal schools, with their playing fields and their farmyards, and tried to reproduce the same atmosphere in their own countries. Bronson Alcott (father of Louisa May Alcott who wrote the famous *Little Women*) was the first American to introduce the Pestalozzi system, at his Temple

*The State Normal School in Albany, New York, was set up by the New York State Legislature in 1844. It was the first college to require a high school diploma for entrance, and the first to train teachers on the college level.*

School in Boston, in the 1830s. That experiment failed. Not until the 1850s did Alcott's assistant, Elizabeth Peabody, succeed in planting the kindergarten or infant school firmly and deeply in American soil.

At the other end of the educational ladder, by 1860 the United States was still some way behind Europe in its conception of the high school and the university. In Europe, though admittedly for only a small proportion of privileged or brilliant youngsters, the German *gymnasium*, the French *lycée*, and the English *public school* (actually a private boarding school) or grammar school took care of precollege education. By contrast, the American high school was still a long way from the powerful and universal system we recognize today.

Above the high school came the college. Sometimes this was called a university. But up to 1860 the United States could boast no true university of the kind to be found in Europe, especially in Germany. A university in the European sense was a place that awarded advanced degrees in theology, philosophy, medicine, and law, and carried on original research. True, after 1815 a number of brilliant young American scholars went to Germany. Most of them were associated with Harvard. On their return they pressed for research facilities, including a much bigger library, and for freedom from the influence of either church or state. Some concessions were made at Harvard, which in company with Yale built up its scientific school. There was a fresh spirit, too, in Jefferson's University of Virginia, which opened its doors in 1825. Virginia was the first American university to break away from the traditional classical curriculum and emphasize advanced study. But until the end of the Civil War, Harvard like other places remained "a college for boys," as Emerson remarked, not "a university for men." Yale, which came out against innovation in a celebrated report of 1828, "the greatest rearguard action in American higher education," lagged even further behind.

Throughout our period the typical college was rural and small. Big cities and big colleges were thought dangerous for young men. The average college had from 100 to 300 students, and from eight to ten professors who taught almost all subjects indiscriminately. Education and morals were strictly regulated. Chapel or church attendance was compulsory. There was a prescribed curriculum, heavily loaded with Greek, Latin, and mathe-

*Yale was America's second university (after Harvard), although it was not formally called one until 1887. This engraving shows some students playing a kind of football on the campus.*

matics, but with room for a smattering of modern languages, and for chemistry and physics and, of course, religion. There were as yet no collegiate sports, and only a few colleges, like Amherst, had gymnasiums. The students, many of them still boys of fourteen or fifteen, released their pent-up energy through religious revivals, literary and debating societies, geological and botanizing expeditions, fraternity antics, hazing, pranks, and occasional revolts against bad food, harsh discipline, or disagreeable teachers. Newer colleges such as Williams, Bowdoin, Amherst, and Union vied with older ones such as Harvard and Princeton in numbers of students and in standards. This education was still overwhelmingly male. Seminary schooling for young women had begun to spread after the Revolution. By the 1830s a few of these seminaries, such as Mount Holyoke, were turning themselves into colleges. Oberlin College, in Ohio, was already committed to admitting students "irrespective of color," and in 1837 admitted women to coeducation with men.

*In 1841 Caroline Rudd (left) was one of the first three American women to be awarded a Bachelor of Arts degree. She studied at Oberlin College, Ohio, and her diploma (below) still hangs in their library.*

*The girls at a female seminary crown the Queen of the May. Emma Willard founded the first such school in Middlebury, Vermont, in 1814.*

91

The new state universities of the West were for the most part coeducational from the beginning. Some, such as Michigan, had ambitious plans. But on the eve of the Civil War, not many women's colleges existed, and the big state university had not yet evolved.

## Growth of the Common School

Putting these facts together, we can see that a good many of the features of American education that we are apt to regard as traditional, even pre-Revolutionary, actually are post-Civil War. What then of the most basic and famous development of all, the common school? Here too practice did not altogether square with theory. Seven of the original thirteen states did not mention education in their constitutions. By about 1800 only the New England states could point to an official system of publicly supported education. Elsewhere, children learned to read and write in church schools, or in charity or pauper schools—much as in Europe. Some states, like Georgia and Virginia,

*While the teacher locks up, children enjoy their play at the end of a day's lessons. With the growth of public schools came a new stress on practical training in education.*

made paper provision for public schools but failed to make financial provision. As late as 1837, well under half the children in Pennsylvania went to free public schools. Virginia did not have a system of public schooling at all levels until after the Civil War. In the South generally, education was neglected except for planters' children. Black children were shut out or discriminated against throughout the Union, although free schools for blacks were established in some states before 1800. Not until 1855, however, did Massachusetts—in so many matters the educational pioneer—declare in favor of integrating the public schools, irrespective of race, color, or creed.

In theory money was available to pay for public schooling. Virginia, for instance, had a state educational fund. Local taxation was levied in New England and New York. Connecticut also relied on revenue from its lands in the "Western Reserve" of Ohio. The Land Act of 1785 had granted one section of public land (640 acres) in every township for the support of schools, as well as two whole sections in each state for the support of higher education. As a result, Ohio and her sister states of the Old Northwest rivalled Massachusetts in educational activity. From the beginning Ohio prohibited pauper schools. The first Indiana constitution laid out a complete pattern "ascending in regular gradations from township schools to a State University." Michigan, even as a territory, adopted a school law based on Massachusetts, and in 1840 Wisconsin too

**NEW-YORK AFRICAN FREE-SCHOOL, No. 2.**
Engraved from a drawing taken by P. Reason, a pupil, aged 13 years.

THE

# HISTORY

OF THE

NEW-YORK

## AFRICAN FREE-SCHOOLS,

FROM THEIR ESTABLISHMENT IN 1787,

TO THE PRESENT TIME;

EMBRACING A PERIOD OF MORE THAN

**FORTY YEARS:**

ALSO

A BRIEF ACCOUNT

OF THE

### SUCCESSFUL LABORS,

OF THE

### NEW-YORK MANUMISSION SOCIETY:

WITH

## AN APPENDIX,

Containing Specimens of Original Composition, both in prose and verse, by several of the pupils; Pieces spoken at public examinations; an interesting Dialogue between Doctor Samuel L. Mitchill, of New-York, and a little black boy of ten years old: and Lines illustrative of the Lancasterian system of instruction.

——•◦•——

**BY CHARLES C. ANDREWS,**

TEACHER OF THE MALE SCHOOL.

——•◦•——

New-York:

PRINTED BY MAHLON DAY.

NO. 376, PEARL-STREET.

..............

1830.

---

*New York established free schools for blacks as early as 1787. Forty-three years later a teacher at the pioneer school compiled a short history containing work from some original pupils.*

approved the Massachusetts system of tax-supported district schools. Yet the states of the Old Northwest persisted in charging tuition to those presumed able to afford it. Connecticut starved its schools of money. Though the law required every town and district to maintain a school, when Horace Mann began his crusade in the 1830s there were over a thousand districts in the state that had no public schools. Even in the most enlightened states the realities of common schooling often fell below the expectations of those who wrote the laws. Henry Ward Beecher was miserable at his school in Litchfield, Connecticut, around 1820:

> It was our misfortune to go to a District School. A little, square, pine building . . . stood upon the highway . . . without bush, yard, fence or circumstance to take off its bare, cold, hard, hateful look. . . . Certainly we were never sent for any such absurd purpose as an education. . . . We were read and spelled twice a day, unless something happened to

prevent, which *did* happen about every other day. For the rest of the time we were busy in keeping still. . . . As for learning, the sum of all that we ever got at District school would scarcely cover the first ten letters of the alphabet.

Young Beecher continued to be wretched until his father put him in a private academy in Amherst, Massachusetts.

## Theory versus Practice

Such stories obviously weaken the claims made for educational progress in Jacksonian America. It would be wrong to conclude that Americans were simply deceiving themselves with fine slogans. Rather, we should look for reasons why educational expansion was easier to prescribe than to achieve.

The first reason, already touched upon, is that there was no tradition of firm control by government—either federal or state. In some European countries education was planned and promoted from the center. In nineteenth-century America the federal government had little involvement in education, and practically none before the

Morrill Act of 1862, which brought into being the new tier of state land-grant universities. By the 1830s, with Massachusetts in the lead, some states were taking responsibility for education. But up to 1860 the state boards of education did not have much power or much money. The driving force came from local communities and from energetic individuals, together with church denominations. So progress was piecemeal and sometimes haphazard.

A second reason is the emphasis on practicality, also already mentioned. This could lead to a contempt for "book learning," especially at the beginning of the period. A self-made man was apt to feel that if he had done well with very little schooling, the next generation did not need it either. Indeed, years in school might make them soft and disinclined to work with their hands. In this light, education might be not only a luxury for a new country but a dangerous luxury. A Texas legislator opposed a bill for a state university in 1856 by saying that such places were "ovens to heat up and hatch all manner of vice, immorality, and crime."

A third reason is that many parts of America were still very thinly populated. Many schools and colleges had to struggle along on low budgets with too few students. Americans were building for the future, but in the meantime often appeared to overreach themselves. Alternatively, with too low a tax base, some areas seemed not to have enough schools. Perhaps they got priorities wrong by founding colleges where improved schools should have come first.

A fourth reason was the nature of American democratic individualism. Parents were usually keen to help their own children. They were willing to pay school fees for this purpose. Often however they did not see why they should be taxed to pay for other people's children. In an era long before state or federal taxes were generally levied, Americans were naturally resistant to almost any form of taxation. Nor were they simply selfish; in rural and poorer areas, taxes for education could be quite a heavy burden. For of course education is never "free": somebody has to pay for it. Parents willing to scrimp for their own children were apt to send them to private academies, and to feel that the district or common schools were not their concern.

A fifth reason, operative in some areas, was reluctance to bring black children into the common school system. This issue was for instance debated in the Ohio constitutional convention of 1850. Certain delegates argued that universal free schooling in Ohio would attract too many Negroes into the state from places like Virginia and Kentucky. On the other hand, they thought it would be both undemocratic and too expensive to set up separate schools for black and mulatto children. Such considerations applied even more strongly in the slaveholding South before the Civil War.

Religion supplies a sixth and final explanation. Common or public schools were by definition open to the children of every taxpaying citizen. America was a religious country. So in principle it was agreed that religion had an important place in the school curriculum. But this principle created problems. Some people, the clergy prominent among them, stressed the fundamental American decision that church and state should be kept separate. A school under state auspices should not, they suspected, give religious instruction. But schooling without religion was liable to produce a godless nation— a prospect to shudder at. Many Americans, Protestant as well as Catholic, felt that "nonsectarian" instruction was so diluted as to be either useless or positively harmful. The main challenge came from the growing numbers of Roman Catholics, especially in New York and New England. Their case was that they were taxed to support public schools which were biased against Catholicism— for example, by using the Protestant Bible and Protestant religious texts. The Catholics claimed that they could not send their children to such schools; they were obliged to set up their own separate "parochial" system. This being so, they wanted tax support for Catholic education. But if that were done, Horace Mann and others argued, the whole idea of the school as a democratic, Americanizing agency would be wrecked. At the outbreak of the Civil War the Protestant-Catholic dilemma remained unsolved. Catholics continued to be taxed on behalf of public schools to which they refused to send their children— except in places where there were as yet no parochial or convent schools.

## Foundations of Future Success

When all these factors are taken into account, American education between 1815 and 1860 falls into fresh perspective. The real point is not that the United States created a perfect system in those decades. The big, dazzling gains came later. Before 1860 some things were perhaps done wrong; others were left incomplete. But the groundwork was laid. In ways not always anticipated, education did promote democracy on the American plan. Thus the tireless propaganda of Horace Mann and other crusaders gradually convinced Americans that the school district and the state were the vital arenas, and that common schooling was an essential idea. By 1860 the idea was accepted though not yet implemented everywhere. Religious leaders had agreed to disagree: in other words, had realized that common schooling must be basically nonreligious, and that the state was the best body to guarantee religious impartiality. The public high school was still taking shape. As late as 1870 over two-thirds of all students entering college were graduates of private academies. But as population increased the day of the high school would dawn.

Mass higher education was still a long way off. In 1900 only about 4 per cent of the population aged between 17 and 22 were at college. But even in 1860 a bigger proportion of young Americans, including women, were going to college than anywhere in Europe. They were not always given a very thorough or sophisticated education. As a rule they had to contend with meager libraries and equipment, and teaching by nonspecialists. Yet students managed somehow—mostly perhaps by teaching each other—to get a pretty good education, if we judge by the results of America's college-trained statesmen, scholars, scientists, and writers. As Samuel Eliot Morison maintains: "For an integrated education that cultivates manliness, and makes gentlemen as well as scholars, . . . and trains young men to faith in God, consideration for their fellow men, service to the community, and respect for learning, America has never had the equal of her little hill-top colleges."

*Under the direction of Henry Tappan, the University of Michigan at Ann Arbor expanded by adding science to its original classical curriculum. This drawing shows the campus in 1854.*

The hill-top college would remain an important American institution. But other developments were in train. There was the imminent transformation of colleges like Harvard and Yale into great universities. There were signs of a similar big expansion among the state universities, particularly in the trans-Appalachian West. Jefferson's dream, the University of Virginia, dated from 1825. In the West, Indiana established a state university in 1821, Michigan in 1837, Wisconsin in 1848. Some, as in Henry Tappan's Michigan, tried to move ahead more daringly than the narrow-minded university regents could stomach. But by 1860 several of them were reaching the takeoff stage.

Another important development in higher education was provision for professional training in law, medicine, and engineering. Up to and even after the Revolution, Americans had gone to Europe for this advanced work. Then the new nation began to create its own institutions. Theology especially flourished. In some respects every college was a theological school, meant to train ministers. In addition, however, each denomination set up its own seminaries. Thus the Unitarians took over the Harvard Divinity School, the Congregationalists that at Andover. The Episcopalians had the General Theological Seminary in New York City and the Presbyterians one at Auburn,

New York. The Catholics, though few in number until the large Irish migration of the 1840s, established seminaries in Baltimore and Boston. The first formal law school, at Litchfield, Connecticut, had been started by Tapping Reeve as early as 1784, and included John C. Calhoun among its alumni. Harvard opened a law school in 1817. When the great Justice Joseph Story of the Supreme Court accepted a professorship of law there in 1829, he soon made Cambridge the center of legal studies in the United States. During this period Americans were still turning to Europe for research in medicine. Yet gradually American medicine caught up with European, and surpassed it in some fields such as dentistry. Two of the big advances of the age are associated with the Harvard Medical School. In 1843 Dr Oliver Wendell Holmes—better known now as essayist and poet—discovered that puerperal fever, which every year took the lives of thousands of women in childbirth, could be prevented by the use of antisepsis. And three years later William Morton first used sulphuric ether as an anesthetic in a surgical operation.

In engineering, the skills required to build canals and railroads, harbors and bridges, and military and naval ordnance were first supplied by the West Point military academy. West Point kept its lead as an engineering school

until the Civil War. But 1824 saw the start of the first private engineering school, Rensselaer Polytechnic. Though modelled on the famous École Polytechnique of Paris, it taught agricultural as well as mechanical science and was thus a precursor of the state "A. & M." land-grant colleges to be founded under the Morrill Act.

All in all, therefore, the American educational scene of the Jacksonian era was busy, varied, disputatious, and optimistic. Americans were not always prepared to foot the bill. They were sometimes suspicious of what might be going on behind the doors of educational institutions. They wanted education to be both spiritual and practical—two things not necessarily compatible. But even their suspicions were a kind of tribute to the power they believed education to possess. Their collective drive ensured that some form of education—a newspaper or a lecture, a school or a library, a stump-speech or a sermon, a law-office or a cheap reprint of a book—was available in every corner of the nation. If they had not finished the play, they had certainly written the first act.

*The United States Military Academy was founded at West Point, New York, in 1802. Many of the engineers who made the transportation revolution possible were trained at the academy.*

# A Churchgoing Nation

When he arrived in the United States in 1831, Alexis de Tocqueville reported: "The religious aspect of the country was the first thing that struck my attention." Other visitors were also impressed with the many outward signs of religious interest and sentiment in the new land. The number of churches was the single item most widely noted in reports of America during the 1830s. Churches seemed to be everywhere—dotting the open countryside, clustering around village greens, and dominating larger communities with soaring steeples pointing heavenward.

Equally impressive was the fact that the churches were so well attended. By 1831, Americans were a churchgoing people. Not all were members—membership requirements were still strict and not lightly assumed. But attendance by the less committed was encouraged by social pressure and community custom. Churchgoing was a badge of respectability. Skeptics as well as believers regarded the churches as bastions of morality, indispensable to the well-being of the republic. As a consequence, at the time of Tocqueville's visit, church attendance averaged three times the membership. There were more churches, more ministers, and more church-goers in American communities than in comparable ones abroad.

Foreigners also noted the self-denying ritual of Sabbath observance in the United States. On the Sabbath, most Americans put aside their work and workday attire to

From the Collection of The Historical Society of York County in York, Pennsylvania

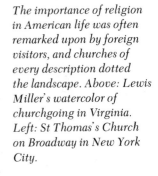

*The importance of religion in American life was often remarked upon by foreign visitors, and churches of every description dotted the landscape. Above: Lewis Miller's watercolor of churchgoing in Virginia. Left: St Thomas's Church on Broadway in New York City.*

Museum of the City of New York

97

make their way to the meetinghouse. They also put aside worldly diversions. They turned away from recreation as well as from work, and spent the day in respectful quiet. Strict observance, to be sure, was never complete. The harborsides of ports and the far edge of the moving frontier were major exceptions. Elsewhere, a few of the profane openly desecrated the day, while the more discreet indulged privately in innocent amusements. Moreover, the continuing attempt to suppress the Sunday mail never met with success. But on the whole, a Sabbath calm prevailed throughout the land.

Even on festive public occasions a show of religion was seldom absent. The Fourth of July celebrations included rough and tumble games, a parade, fireworks, the reading of the Declaration of Independence, and an oration. The parade was led by a fife and drum corps, followed by members of the Society of the Cincinnati (for descendants of Revolutionary War officers) and the local militia. Sunday school children and members of local temperance societies carried banners in the procession. The oration was surrounded with prayers, and the speaker was often a clergyman. Whether given by clergymen or not, the oration usually made use of Biblical themes to set forth the American epic.

There were other indications of a pervasive religious atmosphere. Chaplains began each session of legislative bodies with prayer. Fast days and days of thanksgiving were proclaimed by governmental authority. The evidence of a witness in court who did not acknowledge a belief in

God was regarded as suspect. The primers, readers, and textbooks from which the children were taught reflected and encouraged the religious ethos of the society. In homes, the practice of daily Bible reading and prayer was widespread. Tocqueville was aware of much hypocrisy in this outward show. Yet he concluded that, after all allowances were made, ''there is no country in the whole world in which the Christian religion retains a greater influence over the souls of men than in America.''

Tocqueville's appraisal of the strength and vitality of religion in American life would not have caused any real surprise in 1831. Church leaders were acutely aware that much needed to be done, particularly in the new areas of the West and in the fast-growing cities of the East, before the influence of religion would be fully secure. Still, they rejoiced in all the evidence of new religious life and had confidence in the future.

Scarcely more than a decade earlier, many would have greeted Tocqueville's optimistic report with skepticism. With the winning of independence, most Americans had been caught up in an intoxicating vision of the future. When the exhilaration of the moment was past, however, there were second thoughts. Hopefulness gave way to

*Religious observance was by no means restricted to Sunday and church: the study of the Bible was an integral part of home life. This painting shows the Reverend John Atwood and his family.*

anxiety. This was especially true of many religious leaders, who began to look to the future with gloomy foreboding. The doleful 1798 report of the Presbyterian General Assembly was not untypical:

> We perceive with pain and fearful apprehension a general dereliction of religious principles and practice among our fellow-citizens, a visible and prevailing impiety and contempt for the laws and institutions of religion. . . . Profaneness, pride, luxury, injustice, intemperance, lewdness, and every species of debauchery and loose indulgence greatly abound.

Bishop Samuel Provoost of the Episcopal Church became so discouraged in 1801 that he gave up his episcopal duties. In 1817, a report of the Episcopal diocese of Maryland stated: "Of the fifty parishes which the diocese contains, the greater part are vacant," and of the "more than eighty places of worship, . . . many for years past, except when occasionally visited by traveling preachers, have been occupied by the fowls of the air and the beasts of the field."

## The Question of State Support

In the years prior to 1818, Lyman Beecher in Connecticut fought hard in defense of the few remaining privileges of the Congregational churches. In this way he hoped to deny victory to the forces of irreligion. When his campaign failed in 1818, Beecher was utterly cast down. "I remember," said his son Charles, "seeing father, the day after the election, sitting on one of the old-fashioned, rush-bottomed, kitchen chairs, his head drooping and his arms hanging down. 'Father,' said I, 'what are you thinking of?' He answered solemnly, 'The Church of God.'" Beecher later confessed: "It was as dark a day as ever I saw."

Beecher was typical of New England Congregationalists who believed that state support of the churches was essential. Without it, society would rush headlong to disaster. But after the event, Beecher changed his mind and declared that the ending of state support was "the best thing that ever happened in the state of Connecticut."

One of the things which struck Beecher most forcibly was the new feeling of solidarity which developed among Christians of all denominations. Up until now, the "minor sects"—Baptists, Methodists, and Episcopalians—had "complained of having to get a certificate to pay their tax where they liked" and had aligned themselves politically with the forces of "infidelity." Now, Beecher noted with relief, the repeal of the church rates had removed "the occasion of animosity between us and the minor sects." As a result, "the infidels could no more

Library of Congress

*Lyman Beecher was one of the most influential Protestant preachers of the nineteenth century. His sermons included trenchant attacks on liquor and Roman Catholics.*

make capital with them against us." Indeed, the situation was the reverse. When the state connection was dissolved, many jealousies and antagonisms went with it. In its place came the spirit of cooperation which was to be so characteristic of Protestant churches elsewhere in the country.

Beecher's other happy discovery was that the voluntary status of the churches subjected them to "that moral coercion which makes men work." Hitherto, "our people" had been content with what "our fathers had done," but now they were obliged to discard their lethargy if they were to survive. There were some who felt that ministers had lost their influence by being cut loose from state support. "The fact is," asserted Beecher, "they have gained." By voluntary efforts, they exerted a deeper influence than they ever could when they held the special position in society symbolized by their "shoe buckles and cocked hats and gold-headed canes."

Tocqueville had come to America with much the same view as Beecher had displayed. He had been taught by the philosophers of Europe that "religious zeal . . . must necessarily fail the more generally liberty is established." In America, however, he found the spirit of religion and the spirit of freedom intimately linked. He asked Roman Catholic priests the reason for this surprising state of affairs. To his astonishment, they attributed the "peaceful dominion" of religion in the United States to the separation of church and state.

Antireligious sentiment, so common in European lands,

was minimized by the voluntary status of the churches. When disaffection did occur, instead of joining the ranks of the anticlericals, the normal procedure was for a person simply to transfer his allegiance to a more congenial pastor and congregation. Almost as remarkable was the respect enjoyed by the clergy. They had to prove themselves or perish, depending solely upon their powers of persuasion and the force of their examples. Clergy were regarded with the deference accorded to first citizens on the basis of their ability and character. Ministers frequently exerted an influence greater than that of all but a few laymen. But all this was only true during the 1830s and later.

## The Changing Religious Scene

The gloomy sentiments of many of the clergy during the first decades of independence were caused by the realignment of religious forces. From the beginning, America was a land of many different churches and sects that ultimately came to be referred to as denominations. In the colonial period there were Quakers, Mennonites, Moravians, Lutherans, Dutch Reformed, German Reformed, French Reformed, Schwenckfelders, Roman Catholics, and many more, including a few Jews. Most of these groups were small, almost negligible in number. The big three denominations in 1776 were the Congregationalists, the Presbyterians, and the Anglicans or Episcopalians. There were also many Quakers scattered

throughout the colonies.

By 1815, however, Baptists and Methodists had become the two largest denominations, and they steadily widened the margin that separated them from other Protestant groups. Episcopalians, because of their former attachment to the British Crown, and Quakers, because of their pacifism, were casualties of the Revolution. But what pushed Baptists and Methodists to the fore was the tide of evangelical religion which began with the eighteenth-century Great Awakening.

A Congregationalist, Jonathan Edwards, a Presbyterian, Gilbert Tennant, and an Anglican, George Whitefield, were at center stage in the Great Awakening. But Baptists, offstage in the wings, reaped the greatest harvest. The surge of Baptist growth, beginning before the Revolution, continued unimpeded throughout the war and the decades that followed. Methodists were merely the revivalist wing of Anglicanism until the Methodist Episcopal Church was formed in 1784. From then on, Methodism spread like wildfire both along the seaboard and in the back country areas of the frontier.

There was no centralized control among Baptists. Methodists, on the other hand, had a highly centralized and tightly organized circuit system, with traveling preachers covering wide areas. Contradictory as it may seem, both types of organization were well suited to rapid expansion when coupled with intense evangelistic zeal. But the real clue to Baptist and Methodist growth was their ability to supply large numbers of preachers in areas of growing population. This was in marked contrast to the limited supply of talent in the other

Courtesy of the New-York Historical Society

*Baptists gained many converts from the revivalism of the eighteenth and early nineteenth centuries. Here a group baptism takes place in 1819 in the waters of Hudson River.*

denominations, which restricted the ministerial office to those who had met formal educational requirements.

Baptists were of two minds on the issue of education. The emphasis differed in the North and the South, but even in the North the surge of growth led to a relaxation of standards. Francis Asbury, leader of the American Methodists, claimed that saddlebags were the best school for preachers. Asbury meant that, equipped only with a pocket Bible, a hymnbook, and a copy of the Methodist discipline in his saddlebag, a circuit rider was better prepared for the task of evangelization than someone who had studied the subtleties of theology. Peter Cartwright, the most famous of the frontier circuit riders, made the point more vividly in the advice he gave to a young preacher from New England: "I told him to quit reading his old manuscript sermons and to learn to speak extemporaneously," and that "if he did not adopt this manner of preaching the Methodists would set the whole Western world on fire before he could light his match."

The most characteristically Methodist feature of the American religious scene in the first half of the nineteenth century was the camp meeting. Though neither originated by nor confined to Methodists, camp meetings became a chief symbol of Methodism because Methodists used them more extensively and effectively than other denominations. The camp meeting evolved almost accidentally, growing out of a Presbyterian "sacramental meeting" in Logan County, Kentucky, in 1800. The meeting was quickly recognized as an instrument which could be used to speed the process of conversion. The whole purpose of the camp meeting was to foster a

Library of Congress

Whaling Museum, New Bedford, Mass

*Methodist circuit riders often traveled long distances in pouring rain to bring the gospel to the people (above). But frequently long journeys were made by large numbers of people to religious camp meetings (left) where the oratory of the preacher could visibly affect members of the audience.*

heightened emotionalism. This would help the hesitant to cast aside their inhibitions, acknowledge their bondage to sin, and break through to the joyous ecstasy of a new life in Christ.

The most famous camp meeting was held at Cane Ridge, Kentucky, in 1801, and established the pattern for those that followed. Estimates of those attending varied from 10,000 to 25,000, many traveling great distances to be present. Rude shelters were constructed by each family. Most of these were scattered through the woods, but the initial ones formed a rough circle around the clearing in which the preaching stand had been erected. Here the main throng assembled to listen to the sermons and exhortations of the preachers, which were interspersed with "spiritual songs"—simplified texts with choruses set to lively folk tunes. An open space in front of the stand was reserved for the penitent who came forward to be prayed for as the crowd continued its rhythmic singing. Elsewhere in the grove, other preachers mounted a stump or the bed of a wagon to exhort smaller clusters of people. Thus preaching, exhorting, and singing were carried on simultaneously at different points in the camp, usually far into the night.

"Sinners" were often struck to the ground in emotional spasms. They would twitch, murmur, and cry out. Others would leap and run before falling to turn, toss, and struggle. Then the fallen would rise to their feet and, with tumbling words of ecstasy, relate their experience and praise God for his mercy. Those about them would burst into song. In such a setting, "the traditionally slow cycle of guilt, despair, hope, and assurance" was compressed into a few days or even hours.

Not all agreed with the use of camp meetings. Many Presbyterians were repelled by the din and confusion. At the other extreme, Methodists were unstinted in their enthusiasm. By 1815, camp meetings were being held throughout the country, usually at pleasant locations along the coast or by a river. Eventually, these became permanent camp meeting sites.

## Bringing the Camp Meeting to Town

Looking back, church historians have described the pre-Civil War years as the period when Methodism triumphed in America. By 1820, the Methodists had matched the Baptists in number and they moved steadily ahead to become the largest Protestant group. In speaking of "the triumph of Methodism," however, the term Methodist was used not as the name of a denomination but as a shorthand for a type of religious enthusiasm. Every denomination was influenced by the theological emphases, religious fervor, and revivalist techniques most commonly associated in the public mind with Methodism. Some of

The Presbyterian Charles Grandison Finney began as a frontier preacher. From there he brought the spirit of revivalism to the city, and became the best-known leader of the movement.

Oberlin College Archives

the more exuberant, whose enthusiasm could not be contained within existing churches, formed new denominations of their own. A Presbyterian lawyer-turned-preacher, Charles G. Finney, became the most prominent and influential representative of this religion of the common people.

Finney burst upon the scene in the 1820s. His chief contribution was to bring the techniques and even the theology of the camp meeting to town. Here he used "protracted meetings" lasting several weeks to produce the heightened expectancy, emotionalism, and concentrated social pressure that made the camp meeting so effective. Moving from a series of startlingly successful campaigns in upstate New York to Wilmington, Lancaster, Philadelphia, and New York City, Finney gave his name to the spreading revivals he left in his wake. In 1832, Finney set up headquarters in New York City. Five years later, he accepted responsibility for training Finneyite preachers at Oberlin College in Ohio. In the meantime, he published his *Lectures on Revivals* which became the standard manual for organizing and conducting revivals.

There was strong opposition to Finney's "new measures" revivalism. But in the end, the popular religious enthusiasm that Finney represented emerged triumphant almost everywhere. Lyman Beecher is reported to have said that, if Finney ever invaded New

England, he would meet him at the border and fight him all the way to Boston. Yet it was Beecher himself who was soon to invite Finney to come to Boston.

Political and religious ideas were closely intertwined during these years, and Finney was closely attuned to the popular mood. Methodism in religion and Jacksonianism in politics were expressions of the same spirit. Both exhibited a sturdy confidence in the ability and common sense of ordinary people. The simple, heartwarming, egalitarian gospel of the Methodists had vast appeal to the common folk who had replaced the wellborn and well educated with representatives of their own in places of political power.

Most noteworthy of all was the blending of Methodist and Jacksonian perfectionism. An ardent Jacksonian congressman made this clear when he claimed that spiritual Christianity and political democracy were proceeding not "in parallels but in converging lines— the one purifying and elevating man religiously, the other politically." As the lines converged, he declared, "proclamation can be made that the millennial morning has dawned"— the time of "man's political and religious redemption," the time "when the lion and the lamb shall lie down together." It was a heady, intoxicating gospel, and Jackson's election marked the beginning of a heady, intoxicating time.

## The Search for Perfection

One effect of revivalist activity was to strengthen the reform impulse in American life. Finney insisted that conversion was the beginning, not the end of the Christian life. His intention, he said, was to put people to work. He so energized his converts that new impetus was given to the many voluntary societies devoted to missionary, humanitarian, and reform causes. As the revivals progressed, causes and reforms multiplied. Temperance, prison reform, dietary reform, dress reform, and the establishment of manual labor schools were all directed in one way or another to the perfecting of

*"The Way of Good and Evil"* is the title of this allegorical drawing. The home, the school, the church lead to heaven. The tavern and the prison are stopping-off places on the road to damnation.

society. But for many, the antislavery movement became the one great cause. It deflected interest from other reforms by preempting much of the moral zeal generated by the revivals. The reform impulse, however, had sufficient vitality to push to the fore one other reform project, a drive for women's rights. This was carried forward by women who had gained a sense of liberation through participation in the revivals and reform societies.

An even more striking product of revivalism was the appearance of unusual forms of religious expression. The American environment favored the growth of new groups. Religious experimentation was encouraged by lack of legal inhibition, by absence of any unified ecclesiastical tradition, and by sufficient space to put into practice novel religious beliefs. In this setting, the revivals created an intense hunger for a life free from sin. They encouraged an emotionalism that sometimes took the form of ecstatic visions (often interpreted as new revelations) and heightened expectations of Christ's second coming. While many found comforting assurance in a conversion experience, the revivals left others distraught and torn by anxiety. Among the latter group appeared individuals who were willing to believe new prophets and prophetesses who promised spiritual security, true holiness, and the coming millennium. For some inexplicable reason, most of the new prophets and prophetesses made their first appearance in upstate New York—in "the burned-over district" as it was later called because of the successive revival fires which swept the area.

Two women, Jemima Wilkinson and Ann Lee, both former Quakers, were the forerunners of the new revelation in upstate New York. Both emerged from obscurity through contact with "new light" or "free will" (Wesleyan) Baptists. Jemima was informed, in a trance that her body was possessed by a new spirit, causing her to be reborn as the Public Universal Friend, a kind of female John the Baptist. Ann had similar visions, and her followers claimed that she was Christ in his "second appearing," manifesting the female element in the Godhead. Both formed their followers into communal societies as a foretaste of the millennium, and both stressed the virtues of celibacy and the equality of the sexes. Jemima's community was restricted to her "Jerusalem" above Keuka Lake, New York. Ann Lee's Shakers were more successful in gathering recruits to a strictly celibate life. They established communities throughout much of New England and at several points in New York, Ohio, Indiana, and Kentucky.

John Humphrey Noyes, a Vermonter converted by Finney in 1831, established a quite different perfectionist community. While Shakers believed sexual intercourse to be the source of all evil, others believed themselves "beyond the law" and lapsed into sexual promiscuity as

Oneida Ltd. Historical Committee

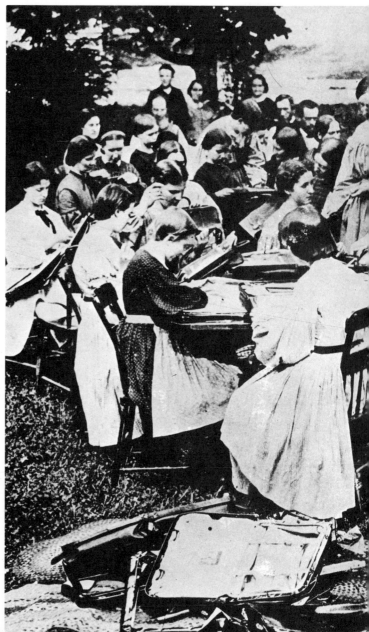

Oneida Ltd. Historical Committee

an expression of the perfect love uniting saints. Noyes rejected such indiscriminate ''spiritual wifery,'' but at his Oneida Community he put into practice a more disciplined form of ''free love'' within the context of what he called ''complex marriage.'' Within the community, each woman was regarded as the wife of each man, and each man as the husband of each woman. Noyes believed that conventional marriage was incompatible with community. ''Sexual communion,'' he insisted, ''differs only in its superior intensity and beauty from other acts of love.'' But when sexual communion is restricted to acts of ''special love'' it becomes unsocial and dangerous to communal interests.

*The leadership of John Humphrey Noyes (left) made Oneida Community one of the most successful and long-lasting of utopian experiments. Below: Members of the community work together. Like most Protestants they believed one of the paths to perfection was through industriousness.*

## The Other Fringe Religions

The membership of these communal societies was small. The more widespread response to Joseph Smith's radical new gospel and new church, therefore, is of greater importance. Smith received a vision of golden plates buried near Rochester, New York. These told the story of a lost tribe of Israel which had inhabited the American continent centuries before. By 1830, he had published his translation of the golden plates as the *Book of Mormon*. In the same year he joined with five friends to ''restore,'' on the basis of a series of new revelations, ''the Church of Christ in these last days'' (that is, the Church of Jesus Christ of Latter-day Saints).

A still different type of religious excitement was provided by William Miller, a Baptist farmer on the Vermont border. While others resolved their doubts and anxieties through new revelations and perfectionist striving, Miller was busy studying the Bible to gain new light and fresh reassurance from old prophecies. The result was a conviction that Christ would return in 1843. His calculations were so convincing that for several years large numbers of people were caught up in the excitement of the expected advent

*Members of the Oneida Community practiced free love or ''sexual communion'' as they called it. Outsiders speculated on the type of interview a new recruit might have to undergo.*

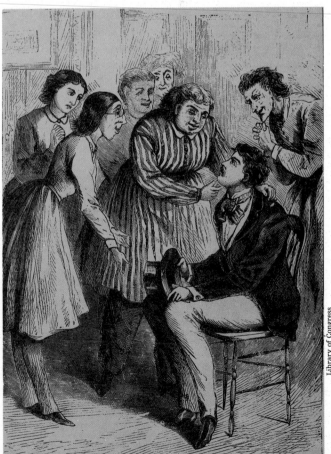

# The Shaker Experiment

The underlying theme of the early nineteenth century Revival was the quest for spiritual perfection, and the Shaker story demonstrates this search. At the height of the Revival in 1826 the Shakers boasted about 6,000 members in eighteen communities and eight different states from New England to Kentucky. Shielded from the sins of the outside world, they chose to live in self-contained communities and pledged themselves to celibacy, communal ownership, industriousness, and confession of sins. God was their king, manifested through the duality of Jesus Christ and their own prophet, Mother Ann.

Ann Lee came from the slums of Manchester, England, a "depraved and odious" city, as she described it. In 1758 she was converted to a radical sect of Quakers called, because of their wild ritualistic dance, the Shaking Quakers, or Shakers. They believed in the imminence of God's second appearance on earth in the form of a woman and in the need for repentance to prepare for this event. Ann Lee zealously preached their message, but on one occasion neither the authorities nor her audience were convinced. She was sent to prison, charged with disturbing the Sabbath.

While in prison, she had a vision and heard the voice of God proclaim her to be the annointed successor to Christ. As the female Godhead, she would complete Christ's work of delivering man from his heritage of original sin. Thereafter, each Shaker would only be responsible for the sins which he himself committed, and could reach salvation through repentance and faith. Released from prison, Ann preached the new gospel, but few welcomed her message. As the persecution mounted against her, she received another divine proclamation: she was to abandon England and spread the faith to the New World.

After a stormy crossing, Mother Ann and eight disciples arrived in New York in August 1774. The first two years were spent coming to grips with the New World, and each of them worked individually in order to make ends meet. Ann herself washed and ironed for a New York household. In the meantime John Hocknell, the man who had financed their crossing, and Ann's brother William Lee explored upstate New York to find a suitably remote tract of land for building. In 1776 they discovered a plot called Niskayuna (later Watervliet), eight miles north of Albany. It was a virtual wilderness of swamp and undergrowth, but they liked its seclusion.

In the early years life was hard. But eventually the small nucleus of believers began to think about expansion. Visitors to the tiny community, impressed by what they saw, spread glowing reports. Word reached the revival meetings in New Lebanon, another upstate village not far away. Then visits took place between the two villages, and soon New Lebanon became the second Shaker village. By the early 1780s it was the Shaker mecca. Hancock, in Massachusetts, was the next community to adopt the Shaker pattern.

Before she died in 1784, Mother Ann named James Whittaker of New Lebanon as the new spiritual leader of the Shakers. Together with his own successor Joseph Meacham, Mother Ann's "first-born son in America," Whittaker codified the rules of the Shaker way of life which combined communalism, confession of sins, celibacy (Mother Ann's idea), and industriousness. After Whittaker's death in 1787, Meacham spent the first twenty or so years of his leadership polishing up the new structure and encouraging the establishment of more communities in New England.

Reasonably satisfied that all was in order in the Northeast, Meacham turned his sights to the frontier. News of the Kentucky Revival had filtered through to New Lebanon, and in 1805 he sent three men on foot to explore the possibilities in the camp-meeting belt. There they began spreading the Shaker message, and soon crowds gathered to hear them on both sides of the Ohio River. Union Village, in Turtle Creek, Ohio, was the first community to emerge—the New Lebanon of the frontier. By 1826, further Shaker communities had sprung up in other parts of Ohio, as well as in Kentucky and Indiana.

Life in all Shaker communities conformed to a very strict pattern. Waking at 4:30 AM (5:30 AM in the winter months), the Shakers each said a prayer and then began their chores. The women cooked breakfast and tidied up the household while the men chopped wood and prepared the fires. By breakfast time, an hour and a half after rising, the households were immaculate. The Shakers ate their breakfast in the same room, but with men at one table and women at the other. Not a word passed their lips. After breakfast they continued to work all day long until mealtime at 6:00 PM with only a short break for lunch. The women did the light work: sewing, tailoring, preparing medicine, educating the children,

*Above: Shakers dance at a New Lebanon meeting. This weird ritual—usually less stylized than is represented here—was central to the Shaker religion. Below left: This Shaker-built barn in Hancock,*

Elliot Erwitt/Magnum

*Massachusetts, exemplifies their passion for simplicity.
Below right: Samples of herbal preparations and
an accompanying cookbook were among Shaker
products sold outside. The Shakers were vegetarians.*

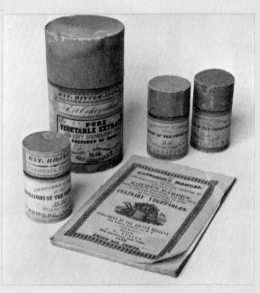

The Bettmann Archive

American Museum in Britain/Derek Balmer

spinning and weaving wool, and cooking. The men worked in the fields, looked after the livestock, built furniture, and designed and constructed most of the communities' buildings.

Although to a large degree self-sufficient, the Shakers did trade with the outside world. And they prospered. Their wares were exquisitely simple and useful, as even "the world's people" could appreciate. The Shakers were also avid inventors, and some of their creations—the wooden clothespin, the rotary saw, the apple peeler, and the wool-braided rug—exemplify their resourcefulness and passion for efficiency.

Their evenings were planned as well as their days. After supper, Shaker men and women filed through separate entrances into the meeting house. Each night of the week there was a specific event. On Monday they might hear the news read, while Tuesday was devoted to a moderated discussion of "the world's" news. Such a discussion was the closest Shakers ever came to small talk. Wednesday there might be a song meeting; Thursday, quiet worship, and so on. But on Sunday the Shakers worshipped throughout the day—with a vengeance.

In fact the most distinctive feature of Shaker life is their worship. No doubt this was a welcome relief from their highly disciplined working life. One eye-witness describes a Shaker Sunday as "a perpetual scene of trembling, shaking, sighing, crying, groaning, screaming, jumping, singing, dancing, and turning." Some of their songs were a form of confession, some a thanksgiving for their gifts: Mother Ann, God, and the ability to speak in tongues. Some Shaker songs would strike non-believers as gibberish; these were a communication with the spirits of the Biblical prophets. When the singing rose to a sufficiently frenzied level, the worshippers would leap into their dance. Some of these dances were stylized, but more often than not they were individual expressions of ecstasy or of "laboring to get good."

The Shakers worked hard to maintain their utopia. But as revivalism waned, recruiting fell off. And of course there was no chance of new Shakers being born into a celibate society. Ann Lee herself had realized that the Shaker way was not an easy one and predicted that "many will set out very fair, and soon fall away; some will go further, and then fall off; some will go still further and then fall; and some will go through. The way of God will grow straighter and straighter; so straight that if you go one hair's breadth out of the way you will be lost."

Three Lions Inc

*Mission fervor was not confined to Protestant sects. Isaac Hecker, a convert to Catholicism, preaches to 10,000 in New York's St Patrick's Cathedral in 1851.*

White Protestantism dominated the American religious scene between 1815 and 1860. But other groups, such as the blacks and Roman Catholics, were also active. Most of the blacks were slaves, but during the pre-Civil War years, "free men of color" were organizing churches of their own. These churches were mostly Baptist and Methodist, and in most respects closely paralleled their white counterparts. Nevertheless, both the preaching and the music had qualities of their own, reflecting a pathos born of their pain, suffering, and indignity. At the insistence of the leaders of these black churches, antislavery sentiment in white churches was redirected from "back-to-Africa" projects to emancipation in America. Instead of deportation, they insisted upon full citizenship at "home." They remained committed to the land which they had helped create, in spite of America's compromised vision and unfulfilled promises.

The other major deviation from the white Protestant norm during this period was the result of immigration. The flood of Irish and German immigrants vastly increased the number of Roman Catholics. Nonetheless, prior to the Civil War at least, the religious tone and character of the country was set by an evangelical Protestantism that owed much to Methodist enthusiasm.

## *The Revivals Decline*

Revivalism reached its peak in the early 1840s. By 1850 most of what Congregational leader Horace Bushnell called the "jump and stir" of the movement was gone. The excitement, with its subsequent disappointment and disenchantment, had taken its toll. The passionate debate on the slavery issue also dampened the optimistic hopes of earlier years. Methodists and Baptists were torn apart by the issue. In 1845, defections resulted in the formation of the Methodist Episcopal Church, South, and the Southern Baptist Convention. The division in the churches was a sign of the political division and civil war that was to follow. Throughout the 1850s, the American people were sobered by the deepening crisis.

There was also the slow attrition that came with the passing of time and the growing prosperity of the churches. Even Methodists were departing from their plain style of life—building costly edifices where the wealthy and fashionable gathered, and "the poor had not the gospel preached to them." Organs were installed and paid quartets were employed to embellish worship services. Camp meetings also had become staid, decorous, and stylized, providing the faithful with an opportunity for a pleasant summer holiday as well as for spiritual renewal. The two most prominent features of the prayer-meeting (or "businessmen's") revival of 1857–58 were its "quietness" and the almost universal approval it received. Scarcely a critical comment was voiced anywhere. The single exception was the outspoken reformer Theodore Parker, who grumpily suggested that the "machinery" which put the revival in motion was "as well known as McCormick's reaper."

Nevertheless, there was a nostalgia for the past. In 1857, Henry Ward Beecher, Lyman's son, was comfortably ensconced in the pulpit of the new and expensively ornate Plymouth Congregational Church in Brooklyn. He was preaching to an ever-growing throng with an eloquence that was gaining him a national reputation. Despite this success, he looked back with some wistfulness to those earlier exciting days in Indiana when he had traveled about as a Presbyterian preacher promoting revivals. Most of all, he lamented the decline of singing in church. "How I long for the good old Methodist thunder," he lamented. "One good burst of old-fashioned music would have blown this modern singing out of the window like a wadding from a gun." But the struggle to make society more perfect had left its mark, and the reform impulse remained strong despite the decline in religious enthusiasm.

# The Reform Impulse

In the spring of 1844, Wendell Phillips, the elegant and eloquent voice of American abolitionism, was addressing a large meeting in Boston. Suddenly, the voice of a woman blared up from the audience like a cracked trumpet to overpower his own. Abby Folsom was once again exercising her God-given right to harangue any audience at any time with her own ideas on free speech and female democracy. The abolitionists had met Abby before. Their only solution was to let her run down (which might take forever) or throw her out. The latter was a delicate assignment for high-minded moralists and pacifists. Nevertheless, Phillips and two others lifted the verbose intruder and gently carried her out of the hall. On the way out, she bellowed that she was more blessed than the Lord Jesus: "He had but one ass to carry him and I have three.". Once outside, she decided that God had been glorified enough for one day, shook hands with her befuddled escorts, and went home.

The incident is significant for what it tells us about American radicals and reformers before the Civil War. The greatest reform movement, the one with the most fateful implications for the rest of American history, was the antislavery movement. In their own time, however, the abolitionists were only one group among many competing for the attention and moral energy of the American people.

Although America has enjoyed a remarkable degree of political stability throughout her history, the roots of the American tradition have periodically been tapped by radicals and reformers of all kinds. Most nineteenth-century reformers believed in the perfectibility of man. Confident that the evils of society could be overcome, almost every protesting group justified itself by pointing to the Declaration of Independence: government is legitimate only when it protects basic human rights. During the first half of the nineteenth century, Americans were still close to their revolution, and an appeal to the declaration carried special power. Jefferson, who had written the document, lived on through the first quarter of the century, and for countless Americans his words carried the conviction of sacred writ. Most men grow conservative with age, but the Jefferson who had advocated revolution as a young man never forsook the vision of his youth. Two weeks before his death in 1826, he reminded his countrymen that the Declaration of Independence placed heavy responsibilities on each succeeding generation:

> May our choice be to the world what I believe it will be, the signal to arouse men to burst the chains under which ignorance and superstition have bound them, so they may assume the blessings and security of self-government. That form of government which we have developed guarantees the unbounded exer-

This scene hand-embroidered on a coverlet satirizes the spirit of feminism. Many men thought the movement for women's rights rather ridiculous; others saw it as a social threat.

cise of reason and freedom of opinion. All eyes are opened or are opening to the rights of man.

Although the American tradition contained the stuff which makes radicals and reformers, the outbreak of idealism and agitation in the second quarter of the nineteenth century was more than a national phenomenon. The roots of evangelicalism and humanitarianism extended across the Atlantic. Leading American reformers during this period were part of an Anglo-American world of humanitarian effort. One is hard put to find any of them who did not, at one time or another, make a pilgrimage to London to confer with brothers and sisters fighting the good fight in England.

Nevertheless, there remains something distinctively American about the radicals and reformers in the new nation. Tocqueville was trying to describe this quality when he called the Americans of Jackson's time "venturous conservatives" who loved change but feared revolution. On the one hand, Americans welcomed the changes overtaking their society and hoped that they would lead the world into a democratic age. On the other hand, the pace of change was so great that they were fearful of losing sight of Jefferson's dream of a virtuous, agrarian republic.

The radicals demanded "freedom now." They insisted that national ideals be turned into realities immediately, no matter what the cost. The conservatives urged caution. They were convinced that, for all its faults, American civilization still represented the greatest achievement of mankind, and they were sworn to conserve what had been accomplished. Many of the humanitarians and reformers of the period found themselves wavering between the desire to change and reform society and the wish to conserve past achievements.

## Radical Voices for the Workers

Early in 1834, Edward Everett, a leading Massachusetts Whig who had married into one of the largest fortunes in Boston, described the contest between Jacksonians and Whigs. To him, it was "nothing more than a war of *numbers* against *property*" which was "to be carried on in the merciless spirit of the French revolution." Everett made these remarks in a letter asking his wealthy Boston friends to raise $100,000 to keep the great Daniel Webster in office. "It is absolutely necessary to meet the crisis with power and means proportional to its terror and the interests at stake," Everett said. He went on to pose an ominous question about the possibility of losing Webster's conservative leadership. "What would have been the condition of public affairs in New England—in the nation at large," he asked, "had Mr. W. taken the side of the levellers instead of the side of security for property and government by law?"

A few weeks later, Orestes Brownson, a leading journalist for the radical wing of the Jacksonians, wrote an essay on "The Laboring Classes." He claimed that the mission of the Democrats to destroy economic privilege, like the struggle against hereditary monarchy and nobility during the American Revolution, would be accomplished only by physical force. "It will come, if it ever come at all, only at the conclusion of war, the like of which the world as yet has never witnessed, and from which, however inevitable it may seem to the eye of philosophy, the heart of humanity recoils with horror."

Although these quotations help us understand the tone of political debate during the Jacksonian period, they grossly exaggerate the radical nature of the Jacksonians. Far from being revolutionaries, Jackson and the people closest to him believed that they had been appointed to carry on Jefferson's work. If they were radical in any sense, it was that some of them, like the New York journalist William Leggett, were willing to take Jefferson's hostility to government power and special privilege to its logical conclusion. Leggett was not only against the special chartering of banks and monopolies, but against post offices, poor houses, and public weighmasters as well, because they would increase the power of government and lead to corruption. He was as much for property as Everett, but he wanted everyone to have an equal chance to acquire it. Like Jackson, his vision of the good society went back to Jefferson; a society in which the yeoman farmer and

Edward Everett, a prosperous Whig from Boston, spoke out against the social changes in Jacksonian America. This portrait was executed by Gilbert Stuart, the famous portrait painter.

artisan are exalted and that government is best which governs least.

Although the struggle between labor and capital was never as desperate as the rhetoric of Everett and Brownson suggests, one of the more radical innovations of the Jacksonian period was the emergence of a politically oriented labor movement. The organization of unions and workingmen's parties was a national phenomenon, but it was particularly strong in the big cities of the Northeast. Apparently the first union to be formed was the Mechanic's Union of Trade Association in Philadelphia in 1827. By the mid-1830s, there were hundreds of unions all over the country and many workingmen's parties.

To many Americans, the prospect of working people organizing politically to protect a class interest different from that of the rest of the country seemed alien and frightening. They would have agreed with the Boston *Courier*'s judgment: "The very pretension to the necessity of such a party is a libel on the community." The fact that similar developments were taking place in England at the same time was cold comfort. Suggesting that rigid class differences of the Old World were beginning to appear in the New simply gave substance to the inflammatory rhetoric of men like Everett and Brownson.

The leaders of the working-class movement during this period have been called "children of the Enlightenment" and "nay-sayers." They were children of the Enlightenment in the sense that they drew heavily on the philosophy of natural rights to show that every man had a right to enjoy the fruits of his labor. They were nay-sayers in the sense that they emphasized not the shining prosperity and promise of America, but the suffering, exploitation, and demeaning status of the working class. The view that workers were losing status in the new industrial system helps to explain why they often said no to Jackson's party. "Once a year they call us men," said one labor leader, "but then they want our *votes,* and they flatter us . . . and it grinds them to the very soul to have their delicate fingers clenched in the friendly gripe [sic] of an honest hand."

## The Fight for Better Conditions

Many Americans obviously had no conception of the working conditions and the quality of life available to mill and factory workers. In 1845, the House of Representatives formed a special committee to hear petitions from women workers in Lowell, Massachusetts, who requested a ten-hour workday. Eliza Hemmingway, a piece-work weaver, testified that her workday began at 5:00 AM and continued until 7:00 PM, with half an hour for breakfast and three quarters of an hour for lunch. The air in the room she considered not to be wholesome, with 354 lamps lit; the fumes were inhaled by the occupants, including children under fourteen years old. All operatives complained of ill health and enforced absences from work without pay. A former overseer testified that, on the contrary, the girls in the mills enjoyed the best of health "for the reason that they rise early, go to bed early and have three meals regular." For eight years, he continued, he had known of only one girl in sixty who "went home from Lowell and died."

*Unions grew rapidly with the development of big cities. Seen here is a membership card for a New York City carpenters' union, one of the earliest to be established.*

*Women work at their looms in a cotton mill. The New England mills were heavily dependent on female labor, and there were many complaints about long hours and bad working conditions.*

The committee listened to the testimony and wrote its report, acknowledging that there were abuses, but concluding that "the remedy is not with us. We look for it in the progressive improvement in art and science, in a higher appreciation of man's destiny, in a less love for money, and a more ardent love for social happiness and intellectual superiority."

In their analysis of what was wrong with America, the labor spokesmen pointed to the bad effects of monopolies, factories, and private property. Like many other Americans, they were ambivalent about economic change. Although quicker than European labor leaders to see the connection between technology and material progress, the Americans complained that the factory system was being used in a way which milked the labor of workers to benefit the wealthy. But they were pre-Marxist critics of capitalism—not opposed to the system itself, but to the way in which it was manipulated to breed inequality.

By the end of the 1830s some of the goals of the labor leaders had been realized: shorter working hours, the repeal of debtor laws, and a growing number of public schools. The workingmen's movement, however, had vanished. It would be more than two generations before unions would emerge again as a force of national significance, and their goals then would be almost exclusively economic. For all the harshness of their rhetoric, the labor radicals shared the values of many of their contemporaries. Their nay-saying was one way of responding to the shocks and traumas of a society undergoing the painful transformation from agrarianism to urbanization and industrialism. By forsaking an appeal to violence, they showed that nay-sayers could still believe that the American system was flexible enough to be made better.

What separated the labor radicals from most other Americans was their belief that problems of poverty, unemployment, and inequality would not be solved by the individual but only by organized cooperative effort. Only

*The use of child labor in manufacturing industries was a social abuse that reformers sought to end. This woodcut shows the scene in a shoemaking factory in 1840.*

in this way could the middle-class majority be forced to begin institutionalizing the promises of the Declaration of Independence.

## Poor Law and Prison Reform

At the same time that the case for the working classes was being argued by labor reformers, the problem of the vicious and dependent classes was drawing the attention of reformers from the middle and upper classes. A substantial part of the moral energy of the period was devoted to ways of providing institutional care for paupers, criminals, delinquents, and the physically and mentally handicapped.

Americans had more difficulty coping with poverty than with problems of crime and delinquency. Back in the eighteenth century, the poor were taken care of in the towns and villages in which they lived, and frequently were put to board in private homes. By the second decade of the nineteenth century, however, this way of treating the poor had begun to break down. Villages grew into towns and towns into cities. With the increasing social and geographic mobility, people in one community frequently felt they were being asked to take care of poor people who belonged somewhere else. One result of this situation was the creation of public almshouses. But genuine compassion for the poor did not develop, nor did the realization that, in a highly competitive society, some people always drop to the bottom and are left behind. The relationship between poverty, crime, and the existence

112

of underprivileged minorities was not widely understood. The Puritan ethic which exalted work, and the democratic ethos which insisted that America was a land of boundless opportunity, encouraged Americans to look on their poor with hostility. The prevailing attitude was that permanent poverty was somehow an indication of bad character.

The same reformers who shied away from the problems of the poor were challenged by the problems posed by criminals and delinquents. Much of the harshness of American penal codes, which during colonial days had employed corporal punishment like ear cropping, whipping, and branding, had been softened during the post-revolutionary period. But there was no formal prison system in America before 1815. Hardened criminals were housed together with debtors, first offenders, juveniles, and sometimes mothers and their children in local jails under conditions which varied with the locality. As the stability of the local communities began to change, leaders looked for a more systematic approach to the problem of handling criminals which would also square with the humanitarian spirit of the age.

It is significant that the first new prisons built in America were constructed near two of America's largest cities. The Auburn and the Eastern State Penitentiaries near Syracuse and Philadelphia attempted to rebuild the prisoner's character by dividing his time into periods of work, Bible study, and meditation. They also restricted his contacts with other prisoners and the outside world to an absolute minimum. The theory was that most criminals had gone astray because, when young, they had not enjoyed the healthy effects of disciplined family life. Reformers believed they could be rehabilitated into productive workers with the mental and spiritual attitudes which society demanded.

It was natural that prison reform should have been accompanied by the recognition that juvenile offenders

*Humanitarian ideals found expression in criminal reform. Above: The model prison near Pittsburgh sought to rehabilitate criminals. Below: Young shoplifters—later reformed in Houses of Refuge.*

*The illustrations above were among several which appeared in an article in* Harper's Weekly *in 1858. They were designed to draw attention to the appalling conditions for prisoners.*

required special treatment. Nothing shocked American reformers more than the breakup of family life, which in large cities like New York put children on the streets to fend for themselves. A girl by the name of Ann, for example, was committed to the New York House of Refuge in 1825. Her mother was a working woman abandoned by the soldier who had fathered the child. Ann had been passed around among relatives and had lived in an almshouse. She had taken to the streets, where she existed by picking up horse chips and stealing coffee, tea, and sugar from the docks to sell to market women. She also ran with a group of juveniles who engaged in pandering and prostitution. She was apprehended by city marshals while going through the pants of a customer ($200 was taken) who was in bed with her colleague. Ann was twelve years old.

The House of Refuge was a part of the "child saving" movement which had become well established in many states by the mid-1820s. Unlike the jail, it concentrated on preparing the child for constructive adulthood. In the Boston institution, for example, children spent four hours in school, five hours learning a trade, and one hour in religious instruction. Tocqueville was astounded to discover how permissive conditions were in the Boston House of Refuge. Youthful inmates were even allowed to run their own system of self-government and discipline.

## Crusade for the Handicapped

The middle-class Americans of Jackson's time who still tended to blame poverty on the poor took a much more humanitarian approach toward the physically handicapped. In 1817, at the same time that Americans were engaged in building new prison systems, Thomas Gallaudet opened a school for deaf mutes in Hartford, Connecticut. In 1831, Samuel Gridley Howe organized the Perkins Institute for the Blind in Boston. His most famous pupil, Laura Bridgeman, had been left deaf and blind at the age of one and a half after scarlet fever. Howe worked closely with her, teaching her to identify objects by utilizing labels with raised letters. He recalled her first rational communication with another human being: "At once her countenance lighted up with a human expression. It was no longer a dog or a parrot . . . it was an immortal spirit, eagerly seizing upon a new link of union with other spirits." Her progress seemed to prove once more the latent goodness and perfectibility of human nature.

Traditional attitudes toward the insane as animals or creatures possessed by demons had been undermined by the rationalism of the Enlightenment. Eighteenth-century physicians like Benjamin Rush in Philadelphia had urged that the insane be treated as sick people, who, like other patients, might be cured. The gradual popularization of this view led to the establishment of mental hospitals in America by the mid-1820s. As late as 1840, however, these institutions remained few in number. Most Americans who were considered insane were confined in jails, poorhouses, or in private care. The plight of the insane was forced upon the American mind and conscience by the work of one woman—Dorothea Dix.

A wellborn New Englander of private means, Dorothea Dix was a person of strong intellect and religious instinct. She spent several years as governess in the Boston home of influential Unitarian minister William Ellery Channing, and later ran a school for girls in her own home. In 1841, while teaching a Sunday school class to a group of women in a house of correction near Boston, she discovered that insane inmates were confined separately in unheated quarters. Her personal investigation of the insane ultimately took her to 18 state penitentiaries, 300 county jails, and more than 500 almshouses over the next three years. She vividly described human beings *"in cages, closets, cellars, stalls, pens! Chained naked, beaten with rods and lashed into obedience!"* In a message to the Massachusetts state legislature in 1845, she told of a young woman at the Danvers almshouse:

> There she stood, clinging to or beating upon the bars of her caged apartment, the contracted size of which afforded space only for increasing accumulations of filth, a *foul* spectacle. There she stood with naked arms and dishevelled hair, the unwashed frame invested with fragments of unclean garments,

*Dorothea Dix was horrified by the plight of the mentally ill. She fought hard to improve their conditions, and her work resulted in the founding of thirty-two hospitals.*

the air so extremely offensive, though ventilation was afforded on all sides save one, that it was not possible to remain beyond a few moments without retreating for recovery to the outward air.

Her appeals to state governments provided the basis for a national campaign for state mental hospitals. By the time the Civil War began, when she became superintendent of women nurses for the Union army, Dorothea Dix had become one of the most celebrated humanitarians in the country.

## Growth of the Temperance Movement

Hard drinking was the rule in America after the Revolution. Rum, whiskey, hard cider, and beer were cheap and plentiful for ordinary farmers and workingmen, and the prevailing belief was that strong drink made strong workers. How the cultivated palates of the wealthy were catered to is suggested by the beverage inventory in Daniel Webster's Boston mansion in 1830. It showed an upstairs room with 3,200 bottles of wine, plus a cellar with two barrels of whiskey, one barrel of rum, and hundreds of bottles of madeira, claret, brandy, and champagne. Webster, like his rival Henry Clay, who was also an accomplished drinker, could say with pride: "It is not often that good wine is under any roof where I am without my knowing it."

Although the private drinking habits of upper-class Americans were scarcely a threat to society, the excessive drinking of the working classes resulted in unbelievable misery and deprivation for many families. Dependent wives with no other resources watched their husbands drink up the family wages, while the example set for their children shocked even the more tolerant citizen. An article from the *Zion's Herald* in the spring of 1835 noted:

> While passing through one of our streets . . . last week we noticed a little boy about ten years old, DRUNK! He lay in the gutter making sundry stiffened gestures, silly and sleepy looks, vociferations, in exact imitation of confirmed low drunkards. After being taken up and falling down a few times, he succeeded in reeling into a grocery, which had been licensed by the *proper authorities* to sell him *as much rum as he wanted!*

It was probably because there was no stigma attached to drinking alcoholic beverages that attempts to promote temperance remained scattered and ineffective. In 1826, however, the traditional tolerance of alcohol was vigorously challenged by the organization in Boston of the American Society for the Promotion of Temperance. The depth and seriousness of the challenge can be measured by the fact that, in the next seven years, the parent organization built a membership of half a million people in 4,000 local societies.

Why did tippling become a monster sin and social evil in the second quarter of the nineteenth century? In the first place, drunkenness ran counter to the evangelical fervor of the age, and some of the greatest preachers of the time, like Lyman Beecher, were among the first to cry for reform. In the second place, the temperance crusade developed during a period of tremendous democratic expansion, when religious and community leaders were concerned with problems of social order. The leaders of the early temperance movement did not come from the working classes, but from the middle and upper classes. Many of them were Federalists who felt threatened by the changes taking place in Jacksonian America and had previous experience in organizations like the Home Missionary or American Tract Societies. These groups were designed not so much to convert sinners into passionate religious enthusiasts as to keep the boisterous common people ''Christian and law abiding.'' In the third place, alcohol began to be perceived as a problem closely related to the other social problems of the day. In 1852, for example, the chief of police in New York City estimated that 5,200 people had been arrested over the past eight years, a ratio of one to every eleven inhabitants.

*Entitled ''The victim of ardent Spirits,'' this lurid cartoon portrays the drunkard's self-destruction. An evil spirit remarks: ''The fellow's stomach has set my wheelbarrow on fire.''*

He attributed these appalling statistics to liquor and the fact that New York then had about 7,000 licensed and unlicensed grog shops.

Finally, temperance leaders were excellent organizers. Their network of paid agents working with state and local societies served as a model for other reform organizations like the American Antislavery Society. In addition, their use of literature and song to spice up their crusades gave them a kind of democratic appeal suitable to the spirit of the age.

Many of the people initially involved in the temperance movement were also involved in other reform movements. ''You couldn't find one abolitionist out of a hundred,'' Wendell Phillips said, ''who was not a temperance man.'' It did not work the other way, however. Authentic radicals in the antislavery and women's rights movements eventually found themselves estranged from their more conservative-minded temperance brethren.

After 1840 the temperance cause was given new life by the organization of the Washingtonian society in Baltimore. Founded by a group of men who had themselves been victimized by alcohol, they were led by an eloquent reformed drunkard, John B. Gough. The Washingtonians preached abstinence the way revivalists preached the gospel, and they extracted a written pledge from their converts. The Washingtonian pledge soon became a badge of respectability for the aspiring middle classes. By 1843, a total of 500,000 pledges are said to have been signed and Americans throughout the country were singing such classic Washingtonian songs as ''The Rum

*Above: A graphic description of the drunkard's progress. Right: "Father, come home" was a constant theme in sentimental temperance literature. Below left: The Pledge—a lifelong commitment to forswear liquor. Below right: The reformed alcoholic spurns Lady Liquor and espouses the chaste Miss Temperance.*

Seller's Lament'' and ''Father Dear Father Come Home With Me Now.''

## The Early Socialist Utopias

''We are all a little wild here with numberless projects of social reform,'' Emerson wrote to Scottish social critic Thomas Carlyle in 1840. ''Not a reading man but has a draft of a new community in his waistcoat pocket.'' He was referring to the scores of utopian experiments then dotting the American landscape. The utopian quest had been an important part of the American experience ever since the Puritans had attempted to turn Massachusetts into a model of civil purity for the rest of the world. During the first half of the nineteenth century, however, utopia was being sought less as a refuge against religious oppression and more as an asylum for those unhappy with the aggressive, materialistic aspects of society.

The most celebrated utopian experiment in America in the first quarter of the nineteenth century was organized at New Harmony, Indiana, by the British philanthropist Robert Owen. Living proof that humanitarianism was not a uniquely American phenomenon, Owen was one of the great success stories of the Indus-

Above: The grandiose plans for the New Harmony community never came to fruition. Below: A glimpse of New Harmony as it really looked. Center: Robert Owen, the Welsh-born founder of the movement.

trial Revolution in England. Unlike other self-made industrial leaders, he never forgot what it was like to be poor. He had long favored laws limiting child labor and regulating factory conditions. He had even built a model factory town of his own in Scotland before coming to America in the early 1820s to establish a socialist utopia.

Owen spent $150,000 of his own money for the property of the Rappites, a colony of German pietists at Harmony, Indiana. Here, in 1825, he set himself up as proprietor of New Harmony, an enterprise which included houses, stores, workshops, and factories. The experiment started with 900 members. Each family was responsible for its own household furnishings and each worker was expected to exchange his or her labor for goods and services from the common store.

In 1826, Owen turned New Harmony into a socialist community. Members shared equally in property ownership and governed themselves through an assembly of all adults. Unhappily, Owen's attempt to translate his theories into practice did not yield good results. The community, which had begun promisingly under his close management, began to falter when left to itself. Parts of the enterprise, like the saw mills and the hat and boot shops, prospered but the textile mills were unsuccessful. Grumbling and dissatisfaction began to develop within the community. At the same time, Owen's radical opposition to such cherished American institutions as family, church, and marriage began to undermine public support for the New Harmony experiment, and these two developments destroyed the early idealism of the community.

In 1827, Robert Owen dissolved New Harmony in a way which gave every financial consideration to individual members and incurred a staggering loss to himself. This "most amiable, sanguine and candid of men," as Emerson called him, returned to England to pursue other reform causes. Whatever else fifty years of liberty had done for the New World, it had not yet created an environment in which large numbers of strangers could work and live together "as a common family."

New Harmony had become a memory long before Emerson's attention was captured by the communes of the 1830s and 1840s, many of which grew out of the transcendental philosophy which he espoused. Emerson taught man to live from within, confident that his own deepest, most profound intuitions came from God. Such a philosophy could encourage an extreme form of spiritual individualism. "No law can be sacred to me," Emerson said, "but my own nature." But it was also antimaterialistic. Emerson and other transcendentalists never tired of criticizing the fact that American individualism was dominated by an obsession for money and success. Always implicit in their criticism was a vision of society in which work, play, worship, and love would complement each other.

## Fruitlands and Brook Farm

There were two conspicuous attempts to turn transcendentalism into utopia, only one of which was even partially effective. In the spring of 1843, Bronson Alcott, a mystic, poet, and iconoclastic educator, who, according to Emerson, "read Plato as an equal," moved with his wife and four daughters to a farm in central Massachusetts known as Fruitlands. The Alcotts were joined by a little band of idealists which included the British reformer, Charles Lane, and Henry C. Wright, a zealous advocate of abolitionism and birth control. Other members were Isaac Hecker, an intellectual New York baker who would later become a famous Catholic convert, and Joseph Palmer, a tough-fisted farmer who had once been jailed for attacking people who ridiculed his beard.

The pilgrims at Fruitlands were searching for "the second Eden" which would "restore man to his rightful communion with God in the Paradise of Good." But as it turned out, the Paradise of Good was beset with serpents. Lane alienated the rest of the community with his dogmatic ways. Alcott and the others were better at philosophizing than farming, and the brave experiment broke down in a matter of months.

All utopias eventually fail, but some fail more quickly than others. Compared to Fruitlands, the Brook Farm community, launched in 1841 at West Roxbury, near Boston, was a success. Brook Farm was the brainchild of George Ripley, a Unitarian minister and scholar of impressive ability. The community which he attracted included farmers, men and women from the skilled working class, and a substantial number of intellectuals and writers including the novelist Nathaniel Hawthorne. It was organized as a cooperative association in which shareholders invested labor as well as capital. No distinctions were drawn between manual and intellectual work.

Because the community was so largely filled with highly educated and talented people, it was known more for its intellectual achievements than for any practical success as a farm. A school combining classical study, art, and music with manual labor attracted students from outside the community. The school was particularly popular with the children of intellectuals in Boston and Cambridge. At the same time, the literary Brook Farmers and their friends found a forum for their ideas in the columns of the *Dial,* the leading transcendental journal in the country.

At the height of its popularity, Brook Farm never numbered more than 100 members. Their objective, as Ripley explained it, was "to prepare a society of liberal, intelligent, and cultivated persons, whose relations with each other would permit a more wholesome and simple life than can be led amidst the pressure of our competitive

*Brook Farm, in West Roxbury, Massachusetts, was the most famous and longest-lived utopian experiment. Josiah Wolcott's painting (complete with rainbow) captures the community's spirit of idealism.*

institutions''. Despite Hawthorne's rather sour treatment of the experiment in *The Blithedale Romance*—he had tired of cultivating his genius by shoveling manure in the barn—the memories that Brook Farm seems to have left with most participants were happy ones. As the notable journalist George William Curtis later recalled, ''The society of Brook Farm was composed of every type of person. There were the ripest scholars, men and women of the most aesthetic culture and accomplishment, young farmers, seamstresses, mechanics and preachers, associated in such a spirit and under such conditions that, with some extravagance, the best of everybody appeared. . . .''

In 1845, the community which had begun as a transcendental enterprise with a strong socialist flavor was organized along more doctrinaire lines according to the theories of French socialist Charles Fourier. For a while, the new Brook Farm (with members divided into ''phalanxes'' defining their special work assignments) flourished and became the showplace for the American Fourierist Movement. But success was short-lived. Membership fell off, and a disastrous fire in 1846 brought the community to the edge of bankruptcy. In 1847, the Brook Farm experiment, which at its best had been, as one member recalled, ''like going to heaven in a swing,'' came to an end.

## Campaign for Women's Rights

Bronson Alcott's famous daughter Louisa May pointed out in her satirical story about Fruitlands, ''Transcendental Wild Oats,'' that the life of a woman in a commune was scarcely different from her life anywhere else. She was required to do ''the many tasks left undone by the brethren, who were so busy defining the great duties that they forgot to perform the small ones.''

Women's place in America was unquestionably in the home. This had been true since the earliest days when English law, which barely recognized women as human beings, had been transplanted to the New World. Married women had no legal rights. They could not own property or make wills. They had no right to their earnings. They could not assume guardianship of their children. Should they inherit money from a deceased husband, then remarry, the inheritance belonged to the second husband. A woman could not, of course, vote or hold office—unless she happened to be a queen.

In 1792, Englishwoman Mary Wollstonecraft wrote a treatise which shocked the world. In *Vindication of the Rights of Women*, she suggested that, aside from biological considerations, there were no differences between the sexes. She demanded that women be educated and give up their foolish subservience. If the Age of Reason proclaimed personal and political liberty as rights, should they be confined only to man?

From the tyranny of man, I firmly believe the

greater number of female follies proceed. I lament that women are systematically degraded by receiving the trivial attentions which men think it manly to pay to the sex, when in fact they are insultingly supporting their own superiority . . . I am scarcely able to govern my muscles when I see a man start with eager and serious solicitude to lift a handkerchief or shut a door, when the *lady* could have done it herself.

Prior to 1845, the American woman had few spokesmen for her rights. In that year, Margaret Fuller, the intellectual transcendental editor of the *Dial* in Boston, published *Woman in the Nineteenth Century.* The style of the small pamphlet is stilted and its statements curiously bland today. But it was the first American statement of women's position and it was loaded with intellectual dynamite. Miss Fuller laid out all of the questions of feminine shortcomings and the reasons for them, then refuted each of the arguments against emancipation. Her goal, she said, was to ''ascertain the true nature of woman; give her legitimate hopes and a standard within herself; marriage and all other relations would by degrees be harmonized with these . . . as a nature to grow, as an

intellect to discern, as a soul to live freely and unimpeded, to unfold such powers as were given her when we left our common home.'' Her views on male and female relationships were indeed radical: ''By man I mean both man and woman; these are two halves of one thought. I lay no special stress on the welfare of either. I believe that the welfare of one cannot be effected without that of the other.''

Miss Fuller's work enjoyed a wide circulation and stimulated a brisk and often heated discussion among intellectuals. But the pamphlet had to fight for table space with dozens of books and magazines exhorting women to hold their husbands in awe, to obey his slightest wish, and to place his comfort and welfare above all else. *Godey's Lady's Book, Peterson's* magazine, Madame *Demorest's* fashion paper, *Sartain's, Leslie's Illustrated Weekly* poured into middle-class homes, helped shape social customs and fashions, and kept women firmly in their place. That place was in the center of the home, surrounded by her children, with her husband's hand—or foot—on her shoulder.

The 1808 *Married Lady's Companion* suggests proper conduct toward a husband:

*Below: A daguerreotype of Margaret Fuller, writer and social critic. Her study of the place of women in society was ''intellectual dynamite.''*

*Below: Women's magazines reflected the view that a woman's role in life was confined to the home. This 1845 illustration is from* Godey's Lady's Book.

As it is your great wish and interest, to enjoy much of your husband's company and conversation, it will be important to acquaint yourself with his temper, his inclination, and his manner, that you may render your house, your person, and your disposition quite agreeable to him . . . Nature has made man the stronger, the consent of mankind has given him superiority over his wife, his inclination is to claim his natural and acquired rights. He of course expects from you a degree of condescension, and he feels himself the more confident of the propriety of his claim, when he is informed, that St. Paul adds his authority to its support. "Wives submit yourselves unto your own husband, as unto the Lord, for the husband is the head of his wife."

Although women's sphere was traditionally the home, husbands generally approved of their wives' participation in good works, and many women added charitable and civic affairs to their family duties. Active in church and temperance groups, women also began attending meetings of antislavery societies and taking increased responsibilities in abolitionist circles.

In 1840, however, American women attending the World Anti-Slavery Convention in London, as accredited delegates, found themselves denied seats merely on the basis that they were women. Opponents of the female delegates used all the traditional arguments to support their point of view, particularly religion. The Bible clearly stated that women were inferior to men, the clergymen argued, quoting St Paul and the Old Testament

freely. They seemed, as Elizabeth Cady Stanton noted, "to have God and his angels especially in their care and keeping and were in agony lest the women should say or do something to shock the heavenly hosts."

The question was hotly debated for an entire day, with eloquent speeches by distinguished American abolitionists. Two of the movement's finest orators, Lucretia Mott and Abby Kelly, were not allowed to speak on their own behalf. Unmoved by the flow of rhetoric, the convention voted overwhelmingly against the women, and they retired behind a bar and curtain, fenced off from the action of the convention.

The women kept silent at the meetings, but among themselves engaged in passionate and indignant discussion. Mrs Stanton met the diminutive Quaker Lucretia Mott for the first time, and the result was an instant recognition of their mutual compassion and concern for mankind—and womankind. They walked and talked for hours in London, discussing the need to educate men to women's potentialities. They lamented the inconsistencies of men who could oppose slavery and still be blind to the needs of women. "They would have been horrified," wrote Mrs Stanton, "at the idea of burning the flesh of the distinguished women present with red-hot irons, but the crucifixion of their pride and self-

*Elizabeth Cady Stanton, Lucretia Mott, and Susan Brownwell Anthony (from left) were in the forefront of the campaign to allow women a greater role in American society.*

respect, the humiliation of the spirit, seemed to them a most trifling matter." Mrs Stanton and Mrs Mott resolved to form a society to advocate the rights of women as soon as they returned home. The action of the convention, far from eliminating the female threat, stimulated many women to new thoughts about their own situations.

## The Seneca Falls Convention

On July 14, 1848, the Seneca *County Courier* announced that a convention would be held that week to discuss the social, civil, and religious condition and rights of women. It had taken eight years before household and family duties made it practical for Mrs Mott and Mrs Stanton to reach this point. Now, they joined with Mary Ann McClintock and Martha C. Wright in making plans for "the inauguration of a rebellion such as the world had never before seen." Searching for the perfect model to express their sentiments, they discarded documents from antislavery societies, peace and temperance groups as too tame. They finally settled on the Declaration of Independence as their guide. The declaration of sentiments presented at the convention followed the exact form of that document, except that "MAN" replaced George III:

We hold these truths to be self-evident: that all men and women are created equal . . .

The history of mankind is a history of repeated injuries and usurpations on the part of man toward women, having in direct object the establishment of absolute tyranny over her . . .

He has witheld from her rights which are given to the most ignorant and degraded men . . . both native and foreigners . . .

He has denied her the facilities for obtaining a thorough education, all colleges being closed against her . . .

He has endeavored, in every way that he could, to destroy her confidence in her own powers, to lessen her self-respect, and to make her willing to lead a dependent and abject life. . . .

The declaration was followed by a series of resolutions calling for action on all these issues, including the right to vote.

On the first day of the convention, the hall was crowded with both men and women. At the last moment, whether through lack of courage, ignorance of parliamentary experience, or native shrewdness, the female leaders asked Lucretia Mott's husband James to chair the meeting. There were speeches, discussions of the declaration and its resolutions, and all were passed unanimously with one exception. The resolution concerned with the right to vote was defeated. Mrs Stanton had insisted on

this resolution over the objection of her husband and Mrs Mott, who said, "Lizzie, thou wilt make the convention ridiculous." The resolution stayed in, however, and it, plus the total number of outrageous sentiments expressed in the document, combined to bring down both the wrath and ridicule of the press on the 100 men and women who signed the declaration. As soon as the storm of antagonism broke in the press, many withdrew their names. But the grievances of women were now made public and the first organized protest against them had begun.

The final resolution of the convention offered by Mrs Mott drew little special attention but it is the most revolutionary statement of all:

Resolved, that the speedy success of our course depends upon the zealous and untiring efforts of both men and women for the overthrow of the monopoly of the pulpit, and for the securing to women an equal participation with men in the various trades, professions and commerce.

Women in America had long struggled for, if not equality, at least some small share in the professions. Antoinette Brown had dismayed Oberlin College authorities by enrolling as a divinity student. Elizabeth Blackwell was refused admittance to dozens of medical schools. Geneva College finally accepted her, but only because the medical students thought it was a joke perpetrated by students of a rival college. Jane Swisshelm was publishing an abolitionist newspaper in Pittsburgh in 1848. She, along with Angela and Sara Grimke and Abby Kelly, spoke widely for the abolitionist cause at a time when well-born women never appeared on a public platform, particularly before a mixed audience. They found that in defending freedom for blacks, they were compelled to defend their own rights to free speech.

## Bloomers and Dress Reform

In advocating freedom for women, more than the right to vote and earn a living was at stake. Amelia Bloomer, editor of the suffragist newspaper the *Lily*, took up the cause of dress reform. The costume which bears her name—a Turkish-style short skirt over full trousers—was actually worn first by Elizabeth Smith Miller. But Mrs Bloomer wore the dress, too, and used the pages of the *Lily* to discuss the costume's merits. Fashionable women's attire, she maintained, threw the spine out of plumb with tight waists and long skirts, heavy weights on the hips, and dangerously high heels. Despite her pleas for convenience and health, the general press had a field day with cartoons and ribald stories about the odd costume.

Mrs Stanton wore the bloomer costume for two years and wrote: "What incredible freedom I enjoyed . . . ! Like a captive set free from the ball and chain, I was always

Punch Library

Punch Library

ready for a brisk walk through sleet and snow and rain, to climb a mountain, jump over a fence, work in the garden, and in fact, for any necessary locomotion.''

The astonishing amount of scorn and ridicule heaped upon the bloomer wearers may have been due in part to the fear that women were indeed freer to move about and further upset the status quo. The bloomer may have been but the outward manifestation of an inner change, deeply threatening to established social customs and male supremacy. In any event, after a few years, most women, including Mrs Stanton, felt that physical freedom did not compensate for ''the persistent persecution and petty annoyances suffered at every turn.'' In 1853, she wrote to Susan B. Anthony: ''I hope, Susan, you have let down a dress and petticoat. The cup of ridicule is greater than you can bear. It is not wise, Susan, to use up so much energy and feeling in that way. You can put them to better use. I speak from experience.''

Mrs Stanton had met Susan B. Anthony two years

*The bloomer revolution inspired a torrent of masculine ridicule. This English cartoon of 1851 reads: ''One of the delightful results of bloomerism—the ladies will pop the question.''*

after the Seneca Falls Convention, and the two women combined their formidable talents to carry the women's movement forward. Unencumbered by family responsibilities, Miss Anthony was the activist and organizer. Mrs Stanton, a fine writer, provided the movement with much-needed educational material, speeches, and documents. It was said of them that Mrs Stanton forged the thunderbolts. Miss Anthony then hurled them into all manner of educational, religious, and political assemblies, to the ''pleasant surprise . . . more often to the bewilderment and prostration of numerous victims; and in a few single instances, to the gnashing of angry men's teeth.''

What elements combined to make 1848 the year of the

declaration? The answers are complex and indeed, perhaps even impossible to ascertain. Certainly the year itself was important, a year of revolution in other parts of the world, when governments were falling and rising, when Karl Marx's *Communist Manifesto* first appeared. In 1848, the New York Legislature passed a law allowing married women to own and manage their own property for the first time. Women had discovered through experience in antislavery societies that they could organize, plan and execute policy, and speak from public platforms. The massive *History of Women's Suffrage*, written by Mathilda Gage, Mrs Stanton, and others, suggests that "Women's discontent increases in exact proportion to her development." Some have pointed out that the movement was the legitimate outgrowth of the American ideal of liberty, taken one step further when women began demanding a share in the new-found liberties. This was the point which the delegates at Seneca Falls were trying to make when they modelled their resolutions on the Declaration of Independence.

## Why Women Rebelled

Possibly sheer practical considerations moved the rebellion forward. In the 1950s, when the southern black lady Rosa Parks touched off a gigantic furor by sitting down in the white-only section of a bus, she was quoted as saying she had no intention of beginning a civil rights struggle. She sat down because her feet hurt and there were no seats in the back of the bus. It is conceivable that many women in the 1840s were moved by similar considerations. For many of them, there was no alternative to revolution. They had to earn a living. They wanted to retain control of their children. They wanted to own their own property, have a right to their own earnings. One of the reasons Mrs Stanton offered for the eventual passage of the women's property law in New York was the pressure applied by rich Dutch families. They wanted their daughters to inherit their holdings, rather than see the family fortunes frittered away by profligate sons-in-law.

Perhaps some women, like Mrs Stanton, yearned for the pleasure and approval of a beloved parent. When she was ten years old, her only brother died shortly after graduating from college with high honors:

> I well remember going into the large dark parlor to look at my brother's corpse, and finding my father there, pale and immovable, by his side. For a long time my father took no notice of me. At last I slowly approached him, and climbed upon his knee. He mechanically put his arm about me and with my head resting on his beating heart, we sat a long, long time in silence. At length he heaved a deep sigh and said, "O my daughter, I wish you were a boy!"
>
> "Then I will be a boy," I said, "and do all brother did."

With little or no encouragement from her family, she studied Greek, Latin, and mathematics. Running to her father with a first prize in Greek, she was crushed when he kissed her on the head, sighed, and said, "Ah, you should have been a boy!" Denied entrance to college because of her sex, she spent dreary years at Emma Willard's school for women, read law books, and continued her self-education throughout her life. She wrote to Miss Anthony in 1855: "To think that all in me of which my father would have felt a proper pride had I been a man, is deeply mortifying to him because I am a woman."

Mrs Stanton died at 87, still dissatisfied with women's lot, with the lack of progress, with the official rhetoric of the movement. In a letter to Susan Anthony in 1859, she lists the chores accomplished that morning—cooking a turkey, a pie, errands, laundry—then laments the death of her father, of reformer friends, and her own dwarfed womanhood. "When I pass the gate of the celestial city and good Peter asks me where I would sit, I shall say, 'Anywhere, so that I am neither a negro nor a woman. Confer on me, good angel, the glory of white manhood so that henceforth, sitting or standing, rising up or lying down, I may enjoy the most unlimited freedom.'"

In 1867 Abby Folsom died. She had been one of the most troublesome of all the eccentrics who used to appear at the great reform conventions of the 1840s. Her refusal to stop talking had made a shambles out of more than one meeting. Abby had seemed to represent everything fanatical and foolish about reformers, and had drawn considerable ridicule down upon their actions. Most people did not know that Abby Folsom, a poor working woman herself, made a practice of nursing drunkards back to health. They did not know that she had once found an insane pauper woman penned in a stall filled with straw and had taken her home, massaged her stiffened limbs, fed her like a human being rather than an animal. After her death, Wendell Phillips reminded his reformer friends that Abby had done more than merely talk.

This could have served as a fitting epitaph for many humanitarians of the antebellum period, whose odd and freakish ways often detracted from their real work. But whether eccentric, radical, or conservative, their accomplishments were relatively small. They focused national attention on the issues, but all the big social and moral problems would reappear after the Civil War. At their best, however, these determined men and women were part of a great tradition which reached back to the religious intensity of the Puritans and the rational optimism of Jefferson, and would extend forward to include other generations of radicals and reformers even into our own time.

*Chapter 5*

# THE CREATIVE IMAGINATION

*In the 1830s American writers and artists still reflected the influence of Britain and Europe. Thus Tocqueville could observe that "the larger part of that small number of men in the United States who are engaged in the composition of literary works are English in substance and still more so in form." Within two decades, however, a uniquely American note had been struck in the work of Nathaniel Hawthorne, Walt Whitman, and others. And in the realm of art, the American landscape came into its own. But though Emerson had called for a break from the influence of older cultures, established styles were widely followed.*

# New Cultural Horizons

In 1818 the noted English wit Sydney Smith, discussing American culture, suggested that there was none. "Prairies, steam-boats, grist-mills are their natural objects for centuries to come. Then, when they have got to the Pacific Ocean—epic poems, plays, pleasures of memory, and all the elegant gratifications of an ancient people who have tamed the wild earth, and set down to amuse themselves—this is the natural march of human affairs." Americans were too busy with the clearing and settling of their continent to turn their minds to the arts and literature. This was understandable, said Smith. But in the meantime, Americans ought not to boast of their meager creative offerings. He went on to ask a series of infuriating questions:

In the four quarters of the globe, who reads an American book? or goes to an American play? or looks at an American picture or statue? What does the world yet owe to American physicians or surgeons? What new substances have their chemists discovered? . . . What new constellations have been discovered by the telescopes of Americans? What have they done in the mathematics? Who drinks out of American glasses? or eats from American plates? or wears American coats or gowns?

The Reverend Sydney Smith was not an ill-natured man. It would probably not have occurred to him that his comments would enrage readers across the Atlantic. The *Edinburgh Review*, the magazine he wrote for, believed in candor. The *Review*'s contributors offered the plain truth, or what they took to be the truth, in place of flattery and hypocrisy. As Smith said on another occasion: "Among the smaller duties of life I hardly know any one more important than that of not praising where praise is not due."

But Americans were hurt and annoyed by the articles referring to themselves that appeared in the *Edinburgh Review* and other influential British monthlies and quarterlies. Here is another example, in the "slashing style," from *Blackwood's Magazine* (1819):

There is nothing to awaken fancy in that land of dull realities. No objects carry the mind back to contemplation of a remote antiquity. No mouldering ruins excite interest in the history of the past. No memorials commemorative of noble deeds arouse enthusiasm and reverence. No traditions, legends, fables, afford material for poetry and romance.

Americans hit back at their European critics. Smith's queries—taunts, as Americans saw them—were still being rebutted thirty or forty years later. By then, of course, his time-scale had been shown to be wrong. The United States did by midcentury stand at the Pacific, and was beginning to make its culture known to the world outside. Even in the era of Jefferson's and Madison's presidencies, Americans were correct to detect a note of contempt in some of the British criticisms.

What hurt most, however, was the sense that if Smith and similar persons were unsympathetic, they were not liars. The United States of around 1820 was not yet able to compete on equal terms with the cultures of the Old World. This was a fact, yet a painful one. So far, there was more promise than performance. Indeed, several American critics were saying almost exactly the same thing as Sydney Smith. They complained that their countrymen were too intent on practical matters to pay attention to art and literature. "To study with a view to becoming an author by profession in America," wrote one disillusioned man, was about as hopeless a project as "to publish among the Eskimos an essay on delicacy, or to found an academy of sciences in Lapland." Horatio Greenough, an extremely intelligent American sculptor, attacked the Europeans for their superciliousness. "Seeing us intently occupied during several generations in felling forests, building towns, and constructing roads," the Old World "formed a theory that we are good for nothing except these pioneer efforts." Europe "taunted us because

*Sculptor Horatio Greenough was keenly aware of the creative dilemma that faced every artist in a new nation. Though born in Boston, Greenough spent most of his working life in Florence, Italy.*

Valentine Museum, Richmond, Virginia

127

there were no statues or frescoes in our log cabins; she pronounced us unmusical because we did not sit down in the swamp, with an Indian on one side and a rattlesnake on the other, to play the violin." But Greenough, who spent most of his professional life working in Italy, was aware of the flaws in his own argument. American civilization, after all, had got a long way past the stage when everybody was cutting down trees or exploring in the swamps. In another essay, Greenough confessed the difficulty of trying to be an artist in a country which was so "deeply imbued" with its bygone heritage of hardworking practicality:

> An American citizen who has gone abroad to study a refined art presents himself before his fellow countrymen at disadvantage. To the uninitiated his very departure from these shores is an accusation of the fatherland. If he sail away to strike the whale on the Pacific, or load his hold with the precious teeth, and gums, and sands of Africa, it is well; but to live for years among Italians, Frenchmen, and Germans, for the sake of breathing the air of high art, ancient and modern, this is . . . thought by many to show a lack of genius, . . . and we are often asked . . . if nature is not to be found here on this continent.

The problem, in essence, was that political independence did not immediately bring cultural independence. Americans felt different from Europeans, and were certain that their political system was vastly better. They might, for the most part, be too busy to bother much about refinements such as poetry and painting. But they did reveal an intense national pride. According to foreign visitors, Americans always wanted to know what other people thought of them—and nearly always expected the answer to be complimentary. Most Europeans shared Sydney Smith's opinion that Americans had a bad habit of bragging about the marvels of their democracy. But this apparent conceit hid an underlying insecurity.

In culture, the United States strove for two different and not entirely compatible things. In order to develop a national identity, Americans yearned for forms of writing, art, and music that would express their own distinct attitudes. They looked forward to the day when such a work would speak to and for Americans, in an idiom that was unmistakably native. They were not sure just what form it would take. But they believed it should somehow convey the atmosphere of American life—the landscape, the variety of citizens, the quality of light under a big sky, the Indian and colonial heritage, the omnipresent *democratic* mood. The trouble with European culture, Americans alleged, was that it mirrored an *aristocratic* society. Something was wrong, and subtly harmful, about the tone of the great bulk of European poetry, drama, fiction, opera, visual art. The famous British historians of the eighteenth century, David Hume being one example, exasperated American readers. They were brilliant but

insidious. So, in the view of America's first great poet, Walt Whitman, were the plays of William Shakespeare. European culture "toadied" to aristocracy. It assumed that kings and queens and glamorous, privileged characters were the proper material of the creative imagination. So were "old, unhappy, far-off things": ancient battles, wicked barons, ruins seen by moonlight. A truly American culture must break away from these conventions. "We have listened too long," said Ralph Waldo Emerson in a rousing lecture of 1837, "to the courtly muses of Europe." American language must capture the vigor and freshness of the kinds of men who had never been to college. "The language of the street," Emerson noted in his journal, "is always strong." He enjoyed "the stinging rhetoric of a rattling oath in the mouth of truckmen and teamsters. How laconic and brisk it is by the side of a page of the *North American Review*"—a good but rather solemn Boston magazine that had started publication in 1815. "Cut these words and they would bleed; they are vascular and alive; they walk and run." *That* was to be the tone of a democratic literature.

The difficulty was that Americans also wished culture to mean something else. In addition to expressing popular democracy, they wanted to achieve a high culture, able to compete with Europe on the same terms. They longed to

*Essayist, poet, and lecturer Ralph Waldo Emerson proclaimed the virtue of the language of the common man. A distinctive American style, he claimed, meant breaking away from European refinement.*

*James Russell Lowell, a leading man of letters, soft-pedaled the idea of a uniquely American cultural viewpoint. This photograph of him was taken by fellow author Oliver Wendell Holmes.*

*A daguerreotype of Henry Wadsworth Longfellow, whose poems enjoyed immense popularity in America and abroad. Many of the characters and themes he wrote about were identifiably American.*

be able to answer Sydney Smith's interrogations with a list of American museums, galleries, colleges, societies for which apology would be unnecessary. They dreamed of the day when American scientists and scholars would be at least on a par with those of Europe; when American writers and artists would be world famous. They hoped to bring to the United States some of the masterworks of the Old World's heritage, and to commission architects who could fill their new cities with handsome buildings in classical or Gothic styles.

## A Collision of Cultural Aims

The two ideas of culture, native and cosmopolitan, collided. Creative Americans often felt this tension inside themselves. Horatio Greenough, torn between the need to benefit from living among other artists and craftsmen in Italy and the passionate desire to establish art in America, admitted that he was "like the ass between 2 bundles of hay." Some of his contemporaries, including the Bostonian poets James Russell Lowell and Henry Wadsworth Longfellow, were apt to deny that there

could be or should be a quite separate American brand of culture. Or at any rate, they did not think its growth could be forced. Lowell mocked writers in magazines who kept insisting that America was a big and a great nation, and must therefore produce a big and a great literature. He said they had the wrong idea of bigness: "If that little dribble of an Avon had succeeded in engendering Shakespeare what a giant might we not look for from the mighty womb of Mississippi! Physical geography for the first time took her rightful place as the tenth and most inspiring Muse."

The vision of a unique American culture was tantalizing but elusive. It was a fine theme for speeches and articles, but until midcentury and even afterward it was more a demand than a reality. In literature, to begin with, the Americans were still users of the English language. A certain number of American words came in: *progress* employed as a verb, a fondness for *fix, guess, reckon, calculate*: these caught the attention of visitors. So did a crop of new words like *disgruntled*, invented at this time as a sort of nonsense language. Otherwise, as late as the Civil War, written and spoken English was remarkably similar on both sides of the Atlantic. Noah Webster, the lexicographer, told an Englishman that by about 1830

129

the Americans had only added about fifty new words to the common tongue. There is a story that during the Revolution a delegate to the Continental Congress suggested that, when the Americans had won the war, they should keep the language and compel the beaten British to adopt another one. This joke points to a fundamental problem for the Americans. In search of a new national identity, they were still obliged to share their speech and literature with a nation they were trying to repudiate. It was as if a child, having grown up, announced to his parents his intention to be totally independent—and then had to live in the old home and compete for use of the kitchen and bathroom with the older generation.

In the same way, nearly all the dominant idioms in music, art, architecture, even fashions in dress, were still European. Arguing that this ought not to be so did not alter the inescapable truth. Actually, in this respect Americans were no worse off than some of the nations in Europe which happened not to be leaders in any particular form of culture. Scandinavians did not feel frantic because their opera came from Italy. Educated Russians

had a positive mania for French culture. The difference lay in the sensitivity of American national pride. They needed to think they could stand on their own feet.

One of the most annoying handicaps for American authors came from the refusal of the United States to subscribe to an international copyright law. Here they saw eye to eye with British authors. Each were protected in their own countries. But in the absence of a copyright agreement, British writers like Dickens were pirated in the United States, and some American authors in Britain. The more reputable publishers voluntarily paid royalties to their foreign authors. A number of less scrupulous ones simply reprinted whatever they wished from abroad. The author received no profit. In consequence, pirate publishers could sell such books very cheaply. Their defense, and that of some ardent American

The Poor Author and the Rich Book Seller, *by Washington Allston. Until 1891, books by Americans had to compete with cheaply produced pirated editions of popular foreign authors. While booksellers profited, local writers did not.*

democrats, was that cheap access to knowledge was the birthright of the common citizen. To pay royalties would be to tax knowledge. This plea was not convincing; the type of literature most often pirated was popular fiction by famous novelists.

On financial balance the United States did better than Britain, since British writers were in general more prominent than their American equivalents. However, if the American public benefited, the American author certainly did not. On the home market, his books had to compete with pirated editions of well-known British writing that sold at half the price. If the price difference had been the other way round, an aspiring American writer might have had a chance to prove his appeal to the American public. As it was, the scales were hopelessly weighted against him. The only way an American could protect his own books from piracy in Britain was to publish them there first, and sometimes to establish residence in Britain. This helps to account for the long periods in Europe spent by Washington Irving and James Fenimore Cooper—America's first two important professional writers. It also tempted Americans to slant their material so as to appeal to a British audience. Favorable mentions by British reviewers brought them prestige in the United States. Once they had crossed the Atlantic, they found that the whole business of writing and publishing was better organized than at home. Irving, for example, who lived in Europe from 1815 to 1832, made his name by producing charming essays and short stories (*The Sketch Book of Geoffrey Crayon, Gent.*, 1819–20; *Bracebridge Hall*, 1822), in a graceful, completely "English" style. His publisher paid him handsomely.

Back at home, the book trade was suffering from growing pains. Until midcentury, publishers in Philadelphia or New York or Boston sold their works only within a limited area. None, as yet, had a nationwide market. They did not have enough capital or scope to pay authors on the British scale. So American writers in this formative era as often as not had to underwrite the cost of their own books. Those who were particularly hard up, such as Edgar Allan Poe and Herman Melville, were at a serious disadvantage. The standard of reviewing, as Poe bitterly complained, was wretched. British reviewers perhaps erred in pulling to pieces work they did not care for. Poe, trying to be equally tough, earned the nickname of "the hatchet man" for his critical articles. The majority of American reviewers erred in the opposite direction from the British. They "puffed" books on behalf of publishers, writing what were in effect advertisements, full of glowing praise. It is worth remembering that even Walt Whitman, America's most original poet of the century, had grown up in this denigrating tradition. When his great work *Leaves of Grass* came out in 1855, Whitman composed a glowing tribute to his book and passed it off as somebody else's review. He cannot be blamed. He and his American coauthors had seen too many books die from sheer neglect.

We can sum up the situation for American culture between the War of 1812 and the Civil War by saying that it was struggling to find a voice and an audience. It was still overshadowed by Europe. Moreover, the educated classes in the United States had a markedly genteel outlook. Most of those who bought books and went to art exhibitions were, above all, anxious to promote "high" culture. They felt threatened by the vulgarity of the man in the street. Some of them were genuinely cultivated people. Others were even more prim than the European middle class. They were easily shocked. They regarded certain French novels as scandalous. They made a fuss because Horatio Greenough's giant figure of George Washington, commissioned for the Capitol in Washington, portrayed him in a Roman toga, seminude. Foreign travelers, sometimes maliciously and inaccurately but with a vein of truth, gave comic instances of American prudishness. The English novelist Captain Marryat spread the story that Americans draped the legs of tables and pianos and called them "limbs" because the word "legs" sounded coarse. If this was far-fetched, there was better evidence for the news that in art galleries where nude sculpture was on show, men and women in America went in to look at different times.

*Horatio Greenough's massive statue of Washington, completed in 1841, made the first president look more like a Roman emperor. The figure's stilted pose and forced grandeur caused much criticism.*

## Visual Arts in America

But this is the bleak side of creative life in antebellum America. To gain a more complete understanding we should emphasize achievements as well as difficulties. Thus in painting, the outstanding first American generation of Benjamin West, Gilbert Stuart, and John Singleton Copley was not quite matched by its successors. For decades to come Europe would exert a tremendous pull on the gifted young American artist—as it had done for the generation of West and Copley. Samuel F. B. Morse, after a precocious success in Europe, went through some dismal years back at home. Like other ambitious painters, he wanted to take big, imaginative themes and paint them on big canvases. Instead, artists of the Jacksonian era were compelled to do portraits—in their opinion a much lower form of art—to make a living. By the end of the 1830s Morse had practically given up painting. He turned his talents to invention—notably the Morse code and the electric telegraph. His career has been presented as a typical failure of the United States to encourage artistic creativity. Morse, we are told, surrendered art to technology.

This is somewhat doubtful. He could, after all, have combined painting and invention if he had been a person of less cranky temperament. Artists were not given lavish patronage in the United States. But then, neither were the mass of artists in Europe. At about the time when Morse gave up painting, the situation in the chief American cities was actually becoming much brighter for the painter who caught the public fancy. Americans were already pouring across the Atlantic as tourists. They came back with renewed enthusiasm for the art they had seen. They formed art associations. When they had enough money, they began to buy works of art for their homes. An appreciative climate was being created. By the eve of the Civil War, a handful of American artists were earning sizable incomes. They were not the men whose names are remembered today. But on their own level they offered an answer to the Sydney Smiths. Theirs was "academy" painting—glossy, skillful, pleasing—and, as such, nearly on a par with the art that drew the fashionable crowds in London or Paris.

Sculpture also aroused interest, and controversy. The members of Congress did not approve of most of the painting or sculpture that they were commissioning for the Capitol. They broke into uproar, however, over Greenough's "Washington." Greenough tried in vain to explain that his aim was to create a heroic figure, half-real and half-legendary. Why, he was asked, depict an American in a toga? Why not? he answered. Americans were willing to build homes, churches, or banks designed to resemble Greek temples. Why should they object to

seeing Washington in symbolic costume? Would they have preferred to have him clad as a general, or perhaps a Virginia planter? Poor Greenough lost the fight. His huge statue, today housed in the Smithsonian, was pushed out into the open air in Washington. Someone who saw it a few years later was half-amused, half-horrified by its vulnerability to practical jokers. A cigar had been stuck in its mouth.

Hiram Powers, another American sculptor who worked in Italy, was much luckier than Greenough. Powers scored a hit with his "Greek Slave," a marble statue that was put on display at the London Crystal Palace exhibition in 1851. It showed a handsome young woman, unrobed, her head bent in what was described as "an attitude of dejection." The viewer was supposed to know that the woman was a captive, on display in a Turkish slave market. A number of Europeans pointed out that the Americans displayed black women in their own slave auctions. But such comment was drowned out by the chorus of approval. Powers was probably the first American sculptor to become famous, and to be admired by foreigners. His countrymen were all the more pleased

The Greek Slave *by Hiram Powers was a great artistic success at London's 1851 exhibition. Although American by birth, Powers spent over half of his life in Italy.*

Corcoran Gallery of Art

because their stands at the exhibition were mostly confined to practical objects. The other nations had contributed all sorts of elaborate *objets d'art*. Powers offset the impression that the United States had nothing to offer but Yale locks and Colt revolvers.

In addition, midcentury American painting began to show an interesting concentration upon a fresh theme: the American landscape. In part, this corresponded to a transatlantic change in taste. But the Americans, especially of the "Hudson River School," seemed at last to be creating a genuine native style. Their forerunner was the English-born artist Thomas Cole, a man of near genius. One of the most fascinating pictures of the Hudson River group is *Kindred Spirits* (1849), by Asher Durand. The two friends of the title are Cole and the New York poet-journalist William Cullen Bryant. They stand together on a flat rock jutting out over a wild landscape. The painter indicates the scene to the poet. Here is a neat representation of the growing together of the creative minds of America. It is also a tribute to an older artist by a younger, and thus an indication of how a continuous tradition was being established. Durand's

*Some Europeans who saw Powers's statue were struck by the irony of an American portraying foreign slavery. This companion piece, "The Virginian Slave," was drawn by Sir John Tenniel.*

career illustrates the stages of growth. He began as an engraver. Then he acquired wealth and friendly patronage, from painting portraits. He was able to afford a trip to Europe, and to take three American pupils with him. On his return, Durand was well enough established to drop portraiture for the landscapes that most fascinated him. He, Cole's pupil Frederick Edwin Church, and the German-trained Albert Bierstadt, helped to give the American public an appetite for paintings of wilderness scenery. Church and Bierstadt traveled widely, and made people marvel at the exactness of their renderings of spectacular mountains or waterfalls. Bierstadt glamorized the Rockies. Church made a sensation with a vast canvas, "Heart of the Andes." Young Mark Twain, who went to see it in St Louis in 1859, stood back and gazed admiringly at the picture through an opera glass, counting the leaves that Church had so painstakingly wrought out of paint.

These three arrived at their vision of landscape by different routes. All would, however, have echoed Durand's main credo: "Go first to Nature to learn to paint landscape, and when you shall have learned to imitate her, you may then study the pictures of great artists with benefit." Not every American artist would have agreed with Durand. But what he was saying accorded with various other American efforts to define a native outlook. The essence of this position, also typified in the outdoor scenes of George Caleb Bingham, William Sidney Mount, and George Inness, was that people ought to rely on their own impressions. An artist needed training, but ultimately he must train himself. Greenough claimed that many of the best painters and sculptors in Europe had told him that "academies, furnished though they be with all the means to form the eye, the hand, and the mind of the pupil, are . . . hindrances instead of helps to art." The academy turned out imitators, young men who got along by reproducing the ideas of their elders. Immense skill was transmitted, but with it a stale whiff of conventionalism.

Greenough's essays were more original than his sculptures. He hit upon a profoundly important rule which was to guide the American creative imagination to a greater and greater extent in future decades. Beauty, to Greenough, was not something added to a subject like a garland. Beauty was, on the contrary, *functional*. An object was beautiful if it did what it was supposed to. As examples he mentioned the clipper ship and the American trotting wagon. Each was built for a purpose: speed. Each was simple, economical, pure: "I remark with joy that almost all the more important efforts of this land tend, with an instinct and a vigor born of the institutions, toward simple and effective organization; and they never fail whenever they toss overboard the English dictum and work from their own inspirations to surpass the British, and there, too, where the world thought them safe from competition." British workmanship, he maintained, was solid, but clumsy

and over-elaborate: "I would . . . beg any architect who allows fashion to invade the domain of principles to compare the American vehicles and ships with those of England, and he will see that the mechanics of the United States have already outstripped the artists, and have, by the results of their bold and unflinching adaptation, entered the true track, and hold up the light for all who will operate for American wants, be they what they will."

American architects were not yet following "the true track" of Greenough's vivid phrase. Or rather, only a handful of pioneers such as Andrew Jackson Downing, an enthusiast for gardens and rural architecture, were pushing forward. But the signs were present. By 1860, American building was beginning to express a distinctive quality in spite of the welter of styles.

## Problems of an "American" Literature

Similar problems and successes can be detected in American literature. There were two generations of authors within the period 1815–60. The first generation, up to the 1840s, faced many difficulties. But in the last years of the 1840s and in the next decade there was a remarkable outpouring of literary genius—an "American Renaissance" as it has been called.

The big three of the first generation were Washington Irving, James Fenimore Cooper, and Edgar Allan Poe, with the poet William Cullen Bryant as a promising lesser talent. Of this trio, Irving became the first American author to earn a substantial income from his craft. He and Cooper won an international reputation while they were still alive. Poe, while less famous, attracted attention abroad, especially in France. All three were productive writers. Irving published short stories, essays, travel narratives, and histories and biographies—including a five-volume life of George Washington. Cooper, best known for his many novels, also found time to write a history of the American navy and some thoughtful accounts of the nature of society in the United States (for example, *The American Democrat*, 1838). Poe, who made his living as a magazine editor, turned his hand to poetry, short stories, one short novel (*The Narrative of Arthur Gordon Pym*, 1838), a long philosophical treatise (*Eureka*, 1848), a number of book reviews, and some important literary criticism. By the test of quality and quantity, the careers of these three pioneering American authors were impressively full.

*Left: Asher B. Durand was in the forefront of the movement that made American landscapes popular. His most famous painting,* Kindred Spirits, *shows artist Thomas Cole and poet William C. Bryant in the Catskill Mountains.*

Each, however, faced problems that he was never quite able to overcome. On the surface, Irving's was by far the happiest life. "Sunnyside," the handsome house he built on the Hudson River north of New York City, was well named. Irving was a jolly bachelor, with many friends on both sides of the Atlantic and hardly any enemies. When the family import business took him to England in 1815 he soon established himself with British painters and writers, among them the famous Scottish author Sir Walter Scott. The leading London publisher, John Murray, brought out his *Sketch Book of Geoffrey Crayon, Gent.* (1819–20). It was an immediate hit, first in Britain and then in the United States. His next two books of essays and stories, *Bracebridge Hall* (1822) and *Tales of a Traveller* (1824), also did well. One tale from the *Sketch Book*—that of Rip Van Winkle—has achieved immortality. For well over a century, readers have been amused and touched by the story of the man who is bewitched by trolls in the Catskill Mountains. Rip falls asleep for twenty years. When he wakes up and goes back to his

*Below: Washington Irving, America's first outstanding writer, wrote mainly for British readers in a predominantly English style. In this engraving he is second from right.*

*Irving's story of Rip Van Winkle inspired a folk opera, a play, and paintings. This oil depicts Rip's return to society after his twenty-year slumber.*

village, everything has changed. Old companions are dead, and so is his nagging wife. The American Revolution has taken place. The village inn sign, which once bore a picture of King George III, now depicts George Washington. Poor Rip is totally confused.

Several other stories by Irving have entered into American folklore. In fact, they were not as original as they seemed. Irving did not have a strong creative imagination, and in any case there simply was no age-old American folk tradition. So he borrowed several of his plots from German or Spanish popular literature, modifying them to fit the American scene. There was perhaps no other alternative, and Irving wrote with such charm that his versions became far better known than the original tales he had adopted. But he paid a price. He stayed in Europe for seventeen years, and went back later for several years more. Though some of his material was given an American setting, his primary audience was British. His success depended on appealing mainly to readers who were not much interested in the United States, and who might even dislike what they thought America stood for. This is the irony of the career of America's first outstanding literary figure. He wrote very

much like an Englishman; his tone was genial, gentlemanly, and rather bland. As a result, he did not manage to set an example of truly native style and outlook that others might have followed. His books even became less popular in Britain. His publisher complained that Irving lacked bite; he was so eager to please that the effect was cloying.

Given his own good-natured temperament, Irving probably could not have done anything else in the 1820s, the decade of his greatest popularity. If he had tried to invent an American folklore entirely out of his own head, the outcome might have been less memorable, and would have been equally artificial. If he had attempted to write in a more distinctively American idiom, which he had no wish to do, he would not have won a large following at home or abroad. In short, Washington Irving— the son of Scottish-born parents—was an early transitional figure. He still thought and wrote more or less as a European. The cultural dominance of the mother country still obliged him to cater to British tastes.

James Fenimore Cooper was a tougher and more ardently patriotic figure. His *Notions of the Americans* (1828) is a robust defence of the ways of his countrymen in face of European criticism. His immortal contribution to American literature is the set of five "Leatherstocking" novels that chronicle the adventures of Natty Bumppo (also known as "Hawkeye"), the simple, courageous, resourceful hunter who tries to live independently in the zone between the Indian tribes and the fringes of white settlement. The sequence, which is not in chronological order, embraces *The Pioneers* (1823), *The Last of the Mohicans* (1826), *The Prairie* (1827), *The Pathfinder* (1840), and *The Deerslayer* (1841). These books cover Natty's life from early manhood in the forest wilderness to his old age and death further west on the open prairie, where he has been driven by the encroaching frontier. It is a great and haunting theme, exploited since Cooper in a host of American (and European) tales of clashes between Indians and white men and of individual heroism set against a wilderness backdrop. Natty is the ancestor of countless later sagas, in fiction and on television, of the fearless, sturdy lone wolf who accepts the best features of both the Indian's and the white man's code but who rejects the tribal barbarities of the former and the greed and the dishonesty of the latter.

Cooper's Indians may be oversimplified. Mark Twain, for one, ridiculed Cooper's picture of their and Natty's skills in hunting and tracking. But Cooper was truly a pioneer in literature if not in firsthand knowledge of forest ways. He hit upon a basic drama, the confrontation between savagery and civilization, which is of timeless significance. He saw the sadness, both for Indians and for freedom-seeking men like Natty, which accompanied the seemingly triumphal march of the American frontier.

## Cooper and Poe—Disillusioned Authors

Cooper was never at a loss for words or, unlike Irving, for plots. He also wrote sea novels, some fantasies such as *The Crater* (1847), and two pieces of satirical fiction, *Homeward Bound* and *Home Found* (1838). Taking his work as a whole, one sees that his standards were actually as gentlemanly as Irving's. He believed in the idea of an American gentleman—well-bred, well-educated, and with a strong sense of social responsibility. In Europe, where he spent several years, Cooper was fiercely democratic. Back in the United States, he came to feel that his country was being ruined by coarse, noisy politicians and newspaper editors. In trying to attack them he lost most of his popularity. Those whom he criticized denounced him as a snob. Cooper, too, in his way, was thus a transitional figure. He thought of the American author as someone like himself—a landowner with a civilizing mission. In Europe such an idea could make sense. In the United States it was increasingly unrealistic. Cooper, we might

*Right: Edgar Allan Poe was deeply embittered by the lack of recognition he received during his lifetime. Only after his death did his verse and horror stories win wide popularity.*

*Above:* The Prairie *was one of James Fenimore Cooper's five "Leatherstocking" novels. Cooper was the first American writer to explore the relation between white pioneer and Indian.*

say, was born too late to feel at home in Jacksonian America. He left behind a splendid legacy, especially the "Leatherstocking" tales. But in old age, embittered and estranged, he was almost ready to believe there was no future for worthwhile literature in the United States.

Edgar Allan Poe developed even more of a grudge against his fellow Americans. In common with Irving and Cooper, Poe thought of literature as something written by a gentleman for gentlemen. But lacking a comfortable income or a family estate, the brilliant Poe had to churn out magazine articles at a killing pace. His poems now and then were praised; "The Raven" was particularly successful. Some of his short stories found favor for their eeriness or their ingenuity. After his death in 1849 at the age of forty, Poe's true originality was recognized. He was, for instance, one of the inventors of the detective story, many years in advance of Arthur Conan Doyle's tales of Sherlock Holmes. But during his lifetime Poe complained that his talents were largely wasted and unrewarded in America. He struck a pose as a southern gentleman (having spent part of his youth in Virginia). As a self-proclaimed southerner he developed a particular grudge against the North. Boston and New York, Poe claimed, controlled the few literary outlets in the United States, and so helped to stifle the creativity of people like himself. He insisted that America should stop trying to imitate Europe in culture. He suggested that short fiction and short poems were the right kinds of literature for the modern age. Here, perhaps, if Cooper was born too late, Poe was born too soon; his ideas later seemed to make very good sense for a quick and bustling nation. He died a frustrated man, half convinced that America did not deserve him.

## Early Triumphs of the American Novel

Cooper and Poe were by no means the last creative artists, in America or elsewhere, to feel that they were unappreciated by their audiences. But by about 1850, a new generation of writers was able to build on the foundations laid by their predecessors. Styles did not change overnight. In Boston, the poets Henry Wadsworth Longfellow and James Russell Lowell, and the poet-essayist Oliver Wendell Holmes, were members of what Holmes called a "Brahmin" or upper-caste society. They and their friends had nearly all received a college education, usually at Harvard. Their tone was gentlemanly and cosmopolitan. They were not convinced of the need for a distinctively "American" literature. English as they had been taught to write and read it was good enough for them. In common with Washington Irving, they did not strive to give their writing an invariably American setting. When the Boston historian William H. Prescott cast about for a

subject, he became intrigued by the Spanish rather than the American past. Narrowing his search for a suitable subject to the Spanish conquest of Mexico by Cortés, he found that Irving was also toying with the same notion. In a gentlemanly way, Irving turned the subject over to him. Subsequently, Prescott showed the same courtesy to fellow Bostonian John L. Motley, on learning that Motley wanted to write a history of the Dutch revolt against Spanish rule in the Netherlands. Prescott was already working on a related topic, but had the generosity to help Motley with his rival project. The greatest of the Boston historians, Francis Parkman, did take North America for his subject, writing some magnificent volumes on the colonial struggle between British America and French Canada. But Parkman, too, was emphatically a gentleman.

The difference between the "Brahmins" and the previous generation was that by midcentury the big eastern cities, especially Boston and New York, had grown greatly in size, wealth, and sophistication. There was now a sizable American audience for polite "culture." Such writers were still, in a way, Anglo-American. Their poems, essays, and histories were widely read in Britain. But as authors they no longer felt so constrained by British rules. When they did choose American settings, there were definite signs now that foreign audiences applauded this Americanness—in part because Cooper had prepared the ground. Longfellow's *Hiawatha* (1855), for instance, may have given as fanciful a picture of American Indians as the "Leatherstocking" tales. But it quickly won a large readership on both sides of the Atlantic. The gentle poetry of John Greenleaf Whittier, the New England Quaker, also struck contemporary readers as both local and universal.

There were, however, some more unmistakably American voices. One of these was the novelist Nathaniel Hawthorne. His words were not at first sight different from those of English novelists of the time. What made Hawthorne different was not his vocabulary but his whole approach. He echoed the concern of other American authors—namely, that it was hard to create satisfactory stories about a country that lacked an ancient past. Sir Walter Scott could draw upon the rich history of Scotland. Charles Dickens could write about the England of his own day because it was so well defined, and because there were so many injustices crying out for attention. Hawthorne's America, by contrast, seemed two-dimensional. Neither the past nor the present stood out vividly. But though Hawthorne said as much, he could in fact look back upon more than two hundred years of New England history. And this past fascinated him, both because it still lived in his bones and because some of its elements, such as the Salem witchcraft trials of the 1690s, seemed puzzlingly remote. Hawthorne lived in the sunshine of an optimistic era. But by temperament he was not a facile optimist. When he looked behind him to

*Above left: Nathaniel Hawthorne was inspired by America's past as well as its present. Above right: An illustration for his greatest novel,* The Scarlet Letter. *Right: Hawthorne's near contemporary, Herman Melville, the author of* Moby-Dick. *Melville had deep insight but was grossly underrated in his own day; his genius was not appreciated until the 1920s.*

the lives of his ancestors, one of whom had been involved in the Salem witch-hunt, he saw dark shadow. Much of his best writing, therefore—several short stories and *The Scarlet Letter* (1850), a story of spiritual conflict set in Salem in the 1640s—delved back into the past. He made psychological drama out of the oddities of human behavior. Guilt, dread, pride, melancholy: these were Hawthorne's abiding interest. Often he dealt with the contemporary American scene, as in *The Blithedale Romance* and *The House of the Seven Gables.* Sometimes his comments were playful. He tried to bring together the daylight and the nighttime of the soul. In his own words, Hawthorne sought 'a neutral ground where the Actual and the Imaginary might meet.'' The aim was not always successful. But at his best, Hawthorne was the most profound, imaginative writer that America had produced. Herman Melville, the American novelist who equalled him in profundity and exceeded him in scope, regarded men like Hawthorne as ''thought-divers.'' They plunged deep and came up gasping, where others were content to splash around on the surface. Melville saw that this apparently "harmless Hawthorne," a shy, awkward person, was unique: neither a Puritan nor a hater of Puritanism, but its first great explorer.

Melville himself was not a New Englander but a New Yorker. Instead of going to college, he went to sea—a whaleboat, he said later, was his university. Young Melville actually sailed to Liverpool and back as a cabin boy before he signed on as ordinary seaman on a whaler bound for the South Seas. Having deserted his ship in the Marquesas Islands, he eventually came back home in a frigate of the US Navy. These experiences at sea formed the basis of his first six books, which came out in a spate beginning with *Typee* (1846) and *Omoo* (1847), and culminating in *White-Jacket* (1850) and *Moby-Dick* (1851). He continued to write busily in the next decade. But readers were more and more baffled by the complexity of Melville's imagination. He was praised as a chronicler of seafaring adventure. Not many of his contemporaries realized that Melville was himself a "thought-diver." What they took for oddity was in later times recognized as the work of an intensely rich mind. His masterpiece *Moby-Dick*, set during a whaling voyage, was the deep investigation of an obsessed person, an indomitable madman, Captain Ahab. Ahab, who pursued the white whale and brought disaster to his entire crew, was both a tough New Englander and a symbolic figure—a demonic hero. *Moby-Dick* and *The Scarlet Letter*, published within a year of one another, were two of the supreme feats of American fiction. Together they proved that the national literature was coming of age, even if the general public did not altogether grasp what was happening.

## In Praise of Individualism

Four years later, in 1855, a book of poems entitled *Leaves of Grass* struck a still more emphatically new note. The author, Walt Whitman, was a New York journalist who had been experimenting with a loose, highly personal type of statement in verse. Whitman's aim was to tell the truth about how it felt to be an American living in the middle of the nineteenth century. His theme was himself, yet he entered imaginatively into the experiences of the mass of his countrymen, white and black, young and old, male and female. Unlike the old Puritans, he did not sit in judgment. He was simply fascinated by the teeming variety of American life styles. He was sustained by an immense faith in the potential worth of ordinary people in a democracy. For the next thirty years Whitman went on revising and adding to his great litany of Americanness. Again, the public tended to ignore him or laugh at him. Along with Melville's, his reputation had to wait until the twentieth century for full recognition. Irving and

Cooper would almost certainly have found Whitman's verse disturbingly vulgar, possibly obscene. The gulf between him and them was a measure of the distance that the American creative imagination had traveled in the space of a generation.

Whitman's poetry was written in the first person singular. He assumed that individualism was the most important feature of life in the United States. Each citizen must speak freely, fully, and honestly. If he were candid and truthful enough, his words would reach other individuals. This, for Whitman, was the essential meaning of community. In his years of experiment he had acquired this outlook from a school of thought prevalent in New England.

Transcendentalism was never an organized movement. It was a body of ideas, by turns practical and mystical, more or less agreed upon by various people living in the Boston area. The chief exponent of Transcendentalist doctrine was the Harvard-educated former Unitarian minister, Ralph Waldo Emerson, whom Whitman spoke

*Walt Whitman's poetry marked a startling departure from previous American writing. His influential* Leaves of Grass *arose, he said, from "absorbing a million people, for fifteen years, with an intimacy . . . probably never equalled."*

Culver Pictures Inc

of as his "master." Emerson lived quietly in Concord, Massachusetts, a neighbor at one period of Hawthorne, and also of his younger associate Henry David Thoreau. Emerson read widely and thought deeply. He set down his thoughts in a private journal, and at intervals he worked his journal-entries up into lectures. These were then published as volumes of essays. Thoreau, too, kept a journal, and transferred parts of it into print. Both wrote poetry in addition to philosophical essays.

Their central creed was the sacredness of the human self. Most people, they felt, never got closer to selfhood than the bad first stage of selfishness. Emerson insisted that inside each individual was a tremendous "unsearched might." "Trust thyself," he urged his fellow men. An honest person might never enter politics, or make a fortune. But he would be fulfilled. His friendships might be few, but they would be permanent. Thoreau, going his own way as a naturalist, was like an intellectual Natty Bumppo. Most men, he remarked, led lives of "quiet desperation." They existed, but they did not *live*.

*Below: The cabin Henry David Thoreau built during his withdrawal to Walden Pond from 1845 to 1847. Taken from a sketch by his sister, it appeared in the 1854 edition of* Walden, *the book about his experiment in "living deliberately."*

*Above: Through his friendship with Emerson, Thoreau was introduced to the Transcendentalist group of writers. For Thoreau the simplest form of living was the most meaningful, and in nature he found contentment.*

Thoreau's experiment in living consisted of two years of solitude and self-sufficiency at Walden Pond. His book *Walden* (1854) is a detailed account of this life. He and Emerson agreed that human beings were happy in proportion to the number of things they could do without.

Whitman drew inspiration from this message of selfhood. For their part, Emerson and Thoreau responded to the basic sincerity in Whitman's poetry. Looking back on the dawning of the "American Renaissance" of the 1850s, it is clear that the national literature was beginning to build upon ideas that have pervaded American writing and art ever since. It has revolved around the self, emphasizing the individual soul, the longing to be free, the quest for personal integrity. This was the distinctive note that began to be heard in the decade before the Civil War. It was not always a joyful or a hopeful note. Sometimes the passion for selfhood brought loneliness and unpopularity. But modern man, as the authors of the American Renaissance intimated, could not escape his destiny. He was a pilgrim, a pioneer, a seeker—a wayfaring stranger.

# Bibliography

## GENERAL

Bode, Carl, *The Anatomy of American Popular Culture, 1840–1861* (Berkeley & Los Angeles, 1959)

*Boorstin, Daniel J., *The Americans: The National Experience* (New York, 1965)

*Branch, E. Douglas, *The Sentimental Years, 1836–1860* (New York, 1934)

*Cunliffe, Marcus, *The Nation Takes Shape, 1789–1837* (Chicago, 1959)

*Dangerfield, George, *The Awakening of American Nationalism, 1815–1828* (New York, 1965)

Ekirch, Arthur A., Jr., *The Idea of Progress in America, 1815–1860* (New York, 1944; repr. 1951)

*Fish, Carl R., *The Rise of the Common Man, 1830–1850* (New York, 1927)

*Gatell, Frank O., & McFaul, John M., eds., *Jacksonian America, 1815–1840: New Society, Changing Politics* (Englewood Cliffs, N.J., 1970)

*Green, Fletcher M., *Constitutional Development in the South Atlantic States, 1776–1860: A Study in the Evolution of Democracy* (Chapel Hill, N.C., 1930)

*Hammond, Bray, *Banks and Politics in America, from the Revolution to the Civil War* (Princeton, N.J., 1957)

*Krout, John A., & Fox, Dixon R., *The Completion of Independence, 1790–1830* (New York, 1944)

*Meyers, Marvin, *The Jacksonian Persuasion* (Stanford, Cal., 1957)

Miller, Douglas T., *The Birth of Modern America, 1820–1850* (New York, 1970)

*Nye, Russel B., *The Cultural Life of the New Nation, 1776–1830* (New York, 1960)

*Pessen, Edward, *Jacksonian America: Society, Personality, and Politics* (Homewood, Ill., 1969)

*Probst, George E., ed., *The Happy Republic: A Reader in Tocqueville's America* (New York, 1962)

*Rozwenc, Edwin C., ed., *Ideology and Power in the Age of Jackson* (Garden City, N.Y., 1964)

*Schlesinger, Arthur M., Jr., *The Age of Jackson* (Boston, 1945)

*Turner, Frederick J., *The United States, 1830–1850: The Nation and Its Sections* (New York, 1935)

*Tyler, Alice F., *Freedom's Ferment: Phases of American Social History to 1860* (Minneapolis, 1944)

*Van Deusen, Glyndon G., *The Jacksonian Era, 1828–1848* (New York, 1959)

Welter, Rush, *The Mind of America, 1820–1860* (New York, 1975)

White, Leonard D., *The Jacksonians: A Study in Administrative History, 1829–1861* (New York, 1954)

*Wright, Louis B., *Culture on the Moving Frontier* (Bloomington, Ind., 1955)

## Chapter 1: A DISTINCTIVE SOCIETY

*Commager, Henry S., ed., *America in Perspective: The United States Through Foreign Eyes* (New York, 1947)

*Cooper, James Fenimore, *The American Democrat* (New York, 1838; new edn., 1956)

Gerbi, Antonello, *The Dispute of the New World: The History of a Polemic, 1750–1900* (Pittsburgh, 1973)

*Grund, Francis J., *Aristocracy in America* (London, 1939; new edn., New York, 1959)

Handlin, Oscar, ed., *This Was America* (Cambridge, Mass., 1949)

*Kraus, Michael, *The North Atlantic Civilization* (Princeton, N.J., 1957)

*Lillibridge, Charles D., ed., *The American Image: Past and Present* (Lexington, Mass., 1968)

*Lipset, Seymour M., *The First New Nation: The United States in Historical and Comparative Perspective* (New York, 1963)

*McShane, Frank, ed., *The American in Europe* (New York, 1965)

*Martineau, Harriet, *Society in America* (London, 1837; abridged edn., ed. Seymour M. Lipset, Garden City, N.Y., 1962)

Stearn, Gerald E., ed., *Broken Image: Foreign Critiques of America* (New York, 1972)

*de Tocqueville, Alexis, *Democracy in America* (2 vols., New York, 1835, 1840; many subsequent edns.)

*indicates paperback

*Weber, Ralph E., ed., *As Others See Us: American History in the Foreign Press* (New York, 1972)

*Westin, Alan F., *et al.*, eds., *Views of America* (New York, 1966)

## Chapter 2: THE ERA OF THE COMMON MAN

Bemis, Samuel F., *John Quincy Adams and the Union* (New York, 1956)

*Benson, Lee, *The Concept of Jacksonian Democracy: New York as a Test Case* (Princeton, N.J., 1961)

*Current, Richard N., *Daniel Webster and the Rise of National Conservatism* (Boston, 1955)

*Eaton, Clement, *Henry Clay and the Art of American Politics* (Boston, 1957)

*Freehling, William W., ed., *The Nullification Era: A Documentary Record* (New York, 1967)

Gunderson, Robert G., *The Log-Cabin Campaign* (Lexington, Ky., 1957)

*Hugins, Walter, *Jacksonian Democracy and the Working Class* (Stanford, Cal., 1960)

Livermore, Shaw, Jr., *The Twilight of Federalism, 1815–1830* (Princeton, N.J., 1962)

*McCormick, Richard P., *The Second American Party System* (Chapel Hill, N.C., 1966)

*Peterson, Merrill D., ed., *Democracy, Liberty, and Property: The State Constitutional Conventions of the 1820's* (Indianapolis, 1966)

*Remini, Robert V., *Andrew Jackson and the Bank War* (New York, 1967)

*Remini, Robert V., *The Election of Andrew Jackson* (Philadelphia, 1963)

Remini, Robert V., *Martin Van Buren and the Making of the Democratic Party* (New York, 1959)

*Sellers, Charles, ed., *Andrew Jackson: A Profile* (New York, 1971)

*Thomas, John L., ed., *John C. Calhoun: A Profile* (New York, 1968)

*Ward, John W., *Andrew Jackson: Symbol for an Age* (New York, 1955)

*Williamson, Chilton, *American Suffrage from Property to Democracy, 1760–1860* (Princeton, N.J., 1960)

## Chapter 3: THE LAND OF OPPORTUNITY

### The Rewards of Industry

*Chevalier, Michel, *Society, Manners, and Politics in the United States* (Boston, 1839; new edn., ed. John W. Ward, New York, 1961)

Cobbett, William, *A Year's Residence in the United States of America* (London, 1818; repr. Carbondale, Ill., 1965)

Fishlow, Albert, *American Railroads and the Transformation of the Ante-Bellum Economy* (Cambridge, Mass., 1965)

*Gates, Paul W., *The Farmer's Age: Agriculture, 1815–1860* (New York, 1962)

Goodrich, Carter, *et al.*, *Canals and American Economic Development* (New York, 1961)

*Habakkuk, H. J., *American and British Technology in the Nineteenth Century: The Search for Labor-Saving Inventions* (Cambridge, England, 1962)

*McGrane, Reginald C., *The Panic of 1837: Some Financial Problems of the Jacksonian Era* (Chicago, 1924)

*North, Douglass C., *The Economic Growth of the United States, 1790–1860* (Englewood Cliffs, N.J., 1961)

Parker, William N., ed., *Trends in the American Economy in the Nineteenth Century* (Princeton, N.J., 1960)

*Saul, S. B., ed., *Technological Change: The United States and Britain in the 19th Century* (London, 1970)

Strassmann, W. Paul, *Risk and Technological Innovation: American Manufacturing Methods During the Nineteenth Century* (Ithaca, N.Y., 1959)

*Taylor, George R., *The Transportation Revolution, 1815–1860* (New York, 1951)

*Thompson, Warren S., & Whelpton, Pascal K., *Population Trends in the United States* (New York, 1933)

### People on the Move (see also list for The Rewards of Industry)

Bartlett, Richard A., *The New Country: A Social History of the American Frontier, 1776–1890* (New York, 1975)

Berthoff, Rowland T., *British Immigrants in Industrial America, 1790–1950* (Cambridge, Mass., 1953)

*Billington, Ray A., *The Protestant Crusade, 1800–1860: A Study of the Origins of American Nativism* (New York, 1938)

*Billington, Ray A., *The Far Western Frontier, 1830–1860* (New York, 1956)

Buley, R. Carlyle, *The Old Northwest: Pioneer Period, 1815–1840* (2 vols., Bloomington, Ind., 1951)

Clark, Thomas D., *Frontier America: The Story of the Westward Movement* (New York, 1959)

*Foreman, Grant, *Indian Removal: The Emigration of the Five Civilized Tribes of Indians* (Norman, Okla., 1932; new edn., 1953)

*Hansen, Marcus L., *The Atlantic Migration, 1607–1860: A History of the Continuing Settlement of the United States* (Cambridge, Mass., 1940)

*Holbrook, Stewart H., *The Yankee Exodus: An Account of Migration from New England* (New York, 1950)

*Jones, Maldwyn A., *American Immigration* (Chicago, 1960)

*Leonard, Ira M., & Parmet, Robert D., *American Nativism, 1830–1860* (New York, 1971)

Pierson, George W., *The Moving American* (New York, 1973)

*Robbins, Roy M., *Our Landed Heritage: The Public Domain, 1776–1936* (Princeton, N.J., 1942; repr. Lincoln, Neb., 1962)

Walker, Mack, *Germany and the Emigration, 1816–1885* (Cambridge, Mass., 1964)

## Chapter 4: A SEARCH FOR BETTERMENT

### Americans in School

*Bode, Carl, *The American Lyceum: Town Meeting of the Mind* (New York, 1956)

Butts, R. Freeman, & Cremin, Lawrence A., *A History of Education in American Culture* (New York, 1953)

*Calhoun, Daniel, *The Educating of Americans: A Documentary History* (Boston, 1969)

*Cremin, Lawrence A., *The American Common School: An Historic Conception* (New York, 1951)

*Curti, Merle, *The Social Ideas of American Educators* (New York, 1935)

Daniels, George H., *American Science in the Age of Jackson* (New York, 1968)

*McCluskey, Neil G., ed., *Catholic Education in America: A Documentary History* (New York, 1964)

Messerli, Jonathan, *Horace Mann: A Biography* (New York, 1972)

*Rudolph, Frederick, *The American College and University: A History* (New York, 1962)

*Sizer, Theodore R., ed., *The Age of the Academies* (New York, 1964)

Thompson, Eleanor W., *Education for Ladies, 1830–1860* (New York, 1947)

*Welter, Rush, *Popular Education and Democratic Thought in America* (New York, 1962)

*Welter, Rush, ed., *American Writings on Popular Education: The Nineteenth Century* (Indianapolis, 1973)

Woodson, Carter G., *The Education of the Negro Prior to 1861* (New York, 1915; repr., 1968)

### A Churchgoing Nation

*Ahlstrom, Sydney E., *A Religious History of the American People* (New Haven, Conn., 1972)

Bodo, John R., *The Protestant Clergy and Public Issues, 1812–1848* (Princeton, N.J., 1954)

*Cross, Whitney R., *The Burned-Over District: The Social and Intellectual History of Western New York, 1800–1850* (Ithaca, N.Y., 1950)

*Ellis, John T., *American Catholicism* (Chicago, 1956; 2nd edn., 1969)

Gaustad, Edwin S., *Historical Atlas of Religion in America* (New York, 1962)

*Hudson, Winthrop S., *American Protestantism* (Chicago, 1961)

*Hudson, Winthrop S., *Religion in America* (New York, 1965)

*Hutchison, William R., *The Transcendentalist Ministers: Church Reform in the New England Renaissance* (New Haven, Conn., 1959)

Johnson, Charles A., *The Frontier Camp Meeting: Religion's Harvest Time* (Dallas, 1955)

*O'Dea, Thomas F., *The Mormons* (Chicago, 1957)

*Olmstead, Clifton E., *Religion in America, Past and Present* (Englewood Cliffs, N.J., 1961)

*Smith, Timothy L., *Revivalism and Social Reform in Mid-Nineteenth Century America* (New York, 1957)

*Weisberger, Bernard A., *They Gathered at the River: The Story of the Great Revivalists* (Boston, 1958)

### The Reform Impulse

*Bestor, Arthur, *Backwoods Utopias* (2nd, enlarged edn., Philadelphia, 1970)

*Blau, Joseph L., ed., *Social Theories of Jacksonian Democracy, 1825–1850* (New York, 1947)

*Brock, Peter *Radical Pacifists in Antebellum America* (Princeton, N.J., 1968)

*Commager, Henry S., ed., *The Era of Reform, 1830–1860* (Princeton, N.J., 1960)

*Davis, David B., *Ante-Bellum Reform* (New York, 1967)

*Flexner, Eleanor, *A Century of Struggle: The Woman's Rights Movement in the United States* (Cambridge, Mass., 1959)

*Griffin, Clifford S., *The Ferment of Reform, 1830–1860* (New York, 1967)

Griffin, Clifford S., *Their Brothers' Keepers: Moral Stewardship in the United States, 1800–1865* (New Brunswick, N.J., 1960)

Harrison, John F. C., *Quest for the New Moral World: Robert Owen and the Owenites in Britain and America* (New York, 1969)

*Holloway, Mark, *Heavens on Earth: Utopian Communities in America, 1680–1880* (2nd edn., New York, 1966)

*Hugins, Walter ed., *The Reform Impulse, 1825–1850* (New York, 1972)

Krout, John A., *The Origins of Prohibition* (New York, 1925)

McKelvey, Blake, *American Prisons: A Study in American Social History Prior to 1915* (Chicago, 1936)

*Schlesinger, Arthur M., Sr., *The American as Reformer* (Cambridge, Mass., 1950)

## Chapter 5: THE CREATIVE IMAGINATION

*Brooks, Van Wyck, *The Flowering of New England, 1815–1865* (New York, 1937)

*Brooks, Van Wyck, *The World of Washington Irving* (New York, 1944)

Callow, James T., *Kindred Spirits: Knickerbocker Writers and American Artists, 1807–1855* (Chapel Hill, N.C., 1967)

Charvat, William, *Literary Publishing in America, 1790–1850* (Philadelphia, 1959)

Flexner, James T., *The Light of Distant Skies: American Painting, 1760–1835* (New York, 1954)

Flexner, James T., *That Wilder Image: The Painting of America's Native School from Thomas Cole to Winslow Homer* (Boston, 1962)

Gardner, Albert T., *Yankee Stonecutters: The First American School of Sculpture, 1800–1850* (New York, 1945)

*Greenough, Horatio, *Form and Function: Remarks on Art, Design and Architecture* (Berkeley & Los Angeles, 1957)

*Harris, Neil, *The Artist in American Society: The Formative Years, 1790–1860* (New York, 1966)

*Huntington, David C., et al., *Art and the Excited Spirit: America in the Romantic Period* (Ann Arbor, Mich., 1972)

Levin, David, *History as Romantic Art: Bancroft, Prescott, Motley, Parkman* (Stanford, Cal., 1959)

*Matthiessen, Francis O., *American Renaissance: Art and Expression in the Age of Emerson and Whitman* (New York, 1941)

*Miller, Lillian B., *Patrons and Patriotism: The Encouragement of the Fine Arts in the United States, 1790–1860* (Chicago, 1966)

*Miller, Perry, ed., *The Transcendentalists: Their Prose and Poetry* (New York, 1957)

Miller, Perry, *The Raven and the Whale: The War of Words and Wits in the Era of Poe and Melville* (New York, 1956)

*Rourke, Constance, *American Humor: A Study of the National Character* (New York, 1931)

*Thorp, Willard, ed., *Great Short Works of the American Renaissance* (New York, 1968)

*One historian has given the title* Freedom's Ferment *to the decades between 1815 and 1860. During those years the common man raised his voice in favor of all sorts of freedom. Some joined the abolitionists; others campaigned for free universal public education, for temperance, for peace, for the better treatment of the sick and the criminal. Some joined Utopian communal experiments. Some urged that women should have the same rights as men.*

*But freedom also included the freedom of the businessman to prosper, the settler to move off into the new western lands, the filibuster to carve out new kingdoms—even the slaveholder to keep his slaves and take them where he wished. Antislavery campaigns clashed increasingly with defenders of the "peculiar institution." There was much dissension over the Mexican War for this reason. Even some of the soldiers involved, such as the young officer Ulysses S. Grant, were apt to consider it an unjust war.*

*However, there was fairly wide agreement that the United States was a special country, acting under God's providence. Here lies the link between the ferment that produced reform and the ferment that produced westward expansion. "Manifest Destiny"—the expression of God's will that the United States should fill out the whole continent of North America—is the subject of Volume 5.*